We are God like Jesus Christ

We are God like Jesus Christ

Emmanuel Okon

ARPress
ILLUMINATING IDEAS
EMPOWERING VOICES

ARPress
45 Dan Road Suite 5
Canton MA 02021

Hotline: 1(888) 821-0229
Fax: 1(508) 545-7580

Ordering Information:
Quantity sales. Special discounts are available on quantity purchases by corporations, associations, and others. For details, contact the publisher at the address above.

Printed in the United States of America.
ISBN-13:   Paperback   979-8-89330-984-3
                eBook   979-8-89330-985-0

Library of Congress Control Number: 2024902447

Contents

INTRODUCTION

I have said that ye are gods, and all of you are children of the most high. (Ps. 82:6)

This particular verse of the scripture happens to be my most favorite scripture in the Bible.

I was fascinated by the fact that God looks at me and feels there is something about me so important that I could be seen as similar, or actually exact, in image and likeness of him.

People look for fulfillment in life in different ways, but I tend to look for it in a very unlikely (ward) place then, because I needed completeness in God. Despite what life has genuinely offered me a fair share of the combination of both ups and downs.

At first, some seem good, but often leave me with frustrated, disappointments, and negative emptiness. Then, I look over to the church for help to fill this vacuum created by God that only He can fill. With all due respect. So many pastors, apostles, teachers, and ministers, through wonderful sermons and teaching, have tried to fill this space, but all to no avail.

Nature and its wonders, only fascinating and full of wonders, could only add more questions than answers to the question, ARE WE Gods?

Did God really mean when He said, **"Let us create man in our image after our likeness"** (Gen. 1:26)?

More so, is Genesis 1:27: **"In His image and likeness created he *** them both male and female"**—I ponder regularly on this truth, which was then a fact. I decided to personally pray, research, and question so many people, researches, summons, and other endeavors.

Well, this book is a product of years of hard work, smart work, especially the grace of God and the encouragement of the Holy Spirit.

This is a journey that you will never regret a leap to discover who God is, who you are to God, and what you have lost for years is about to be regained. ENJOY.

Chapter 1

What Gods Do to Remain Gods?

GODS MUST WITNESS CHRIST

Witness: Watch, observe, notice, spectator, onlooker, eyewitness

Witness can be defined as (1) attesting of a fact evidence testimony, and (2) a person who saw and give a firsthand account of something or event.

As believers, we all qualify to be called to attest to the fact that Jesus is real and give evidence of this testimony. I am a reality and an evidence that Jesus lives, died, and was raised from death. I live because Christ lives. I reign because Jesus reigns.

Please, let me say this: I am not just a spectator, onlooker, but rather a participant of the great and wonderful project and plan of God, which was done through Christ.

It is your duty to witness and follow Jesus. Jesus said to Peter after the great catch, **Come follow me, Jesus said and I will make you fishers of men.** (Matt. 4:19)

Fishers of men, he says. Jesus has given these shocked but frustrated fishermen a new employment. He used the verb they were used to, i.e., fishing, to illustrate a new vocation, without changing the methodology of fishing. But only the commodity this time is different. Instead of fish, Jesus replaced it with men.

World (humanity)—the work of fishing entails a lot of handwork, risk, personal sacrifice, adventure, and sometimes frustration. But with the miracle they just WITNESSED, it appeared this was their real time for a change, and they couldn't refuse the offer of a better life with this miracle-working man with the assurance and promise of a better life, both in this world and in the world to come.

Jesus gave this great commission to all believers when he said,

Go ye into the world and preach the good news to all creation. (Mark 16:15)

All believers have been sent forth with a mandate to witness as firsthand eyewitnesses. As gods, we hold a better conviction because we witness, because we know, and for sure, because it has happened to us. The change is evident and documented.

OUR SCOPE OF WITNESSING AND OUR LOCATION

The master, our master, said as regard our scope is this:

Go ye into the world and reach the gospel.

The world is our platform; the entire earth should be covered according to that statement. Therefore, we have no boundaries, neither do we have any kind of problem. All we need is faith and the boldness to rise up and go. Hallelujah.

Go ye therefore and teach all nations. Baptizing them in the name of the father and of the son and of the Holy Spirit. (Mark 28:19)

We are mandated to teach all nations—Islamic, Jewish, Christian, Catholic, Pagans, or north, south, eastern religious countries, like China, Korea, Japan, Russia, etc. African nations are not left out in this project. Wherever humans exist, Jesus told us to go there and preach the good news. He also said,

WHAT WE SHOULD TEACH AND PREACH

The gospel will inform them of forgiveness of their sins

And repentance and forgiveness of sins will be preached in his name to all nations beginning in Jerusalem. (Luke 24:47)

God is specific about what we should witness, and that is repentance and forgiveness. This is because all mankind sinned, and the judgment was death in only one name. The name of Jesus alone is salvation and redemption. Also, we are asked to preach the kingdom of God.

And he sent them out to preach the kingdom of God and to heal the sick. (Luke 9:2)

God sent Jesus, and He sent us to talk about our belief.

What we know:

I tell you the truth, we speak of what we know and testify to what we have seen. (John 3:11)

Also, **We speak the things which we have seen and heard.** (Act 4:20)

WHY DO WE NEED TO WITNESS?

1. SAVE SOULS FROM DEATH

    A true witness delivereth souls. (Prov. 14:25)

    When we preach, souls are delivered from hell

2. To also **open their eyes, and to turn from power of darkness to light and power of Satan unto God.** (Act 26:18)

    The god of the world, Satan, had blinded the eyes of the inhabitants of the earth, so Jesus asked us to go and open their physical and spiritual eyes.

3. Convert sinners:

    Remember this, whoever turns a sinner from the error of his way save him from death and cover over a multitude of sins. (James 5:20)

4. We witness to show that we are not ashamed of Jesus:

    If anyone is ashamed of me and my words on these Adulterous and sinful generation. The son of man will be ashamed of him when he comes in his father's glory with the holy angels. (Mark 8:28)

5. We preach so we don't deny him.

    He said, **I tell you whosoever acknowledge me before man, the son of man will also acknowledge him before the holy angels of God. But he who disowns me before men, will be disowned before the angels of God.** (Luke 12:8–9)

6. We witness to avert a curse of not doing so.

    Yet when I preach the gospel I cannot boast, for I am

compelled to preach Woe to me if I do not preach the gospel.

7. We preach because so many people are lost.

   And even if our gospel is veiled, it is veiled to those who are (lost) perishing. (2 Cor. 4:3)

8. We preach to gather together those predestinated.

   For whom he died foreknow he also died predestinate to be conformed to the image of his son... Moreover, whom he died predestinate, them he also called, them he also called and whom he called them he also justified, and whom he justified them he also glorified. (Rom. 8:29A–30)

WITNESSING USING THE WORD MAKES US EFFECTIVE AND YIELD RESULTS

The word is very powerful and convinces people better and faster. This is because the Word of God is a spirit, and the spirit is a better witness than everybody put together.

1. The Word of God is therefore potent:

   They taught through Judah taking with them the book of law of the lord; they went around to all the towns of Judah and taught the people. (2 Chron. 17:9)

2. The scripture testifies of Jesus:

   You diligently study the scriptures because you think that by them you possess eternal life. These are the scriptures that testify about me. (John 5:39)

3. To convince your hearers:

   For he vigorously related the Jews in public debate; proving from the scriptures that Jesu was the Christ. (Acts 18:28)

4. Answers words of truth:

   Pay attention and listen to the sayings of the wise apply your heart to what I teach. (Prov. 22:17)

   So that your trust may be in the lord. I teach you today even you. (Prov. 22:19)

   That I may make thee know the certainty of the words of truth, that thou mightiest answer the words of truth to them that send unto thee. (Prov. 22:21)

5. We preach because it is good for exhorts, reproof, and rebuke.

Preach the word; be instant in season, out of season, reprove, rebuke, exhort with all long-suffering and doctrine.

What do gods preach or witness?

Witness to people as commanded by our Lord, Jesus, on daily basis. We are mandated to preach the following:

1. Christ crucified.

    We preach Christ crucified unto the Jews a stumbling block, and unto the Greeks foolishness. (1 Cor. 1:23)

2. Christ died for our sins.

    For I delivered unto you first of all that which I also received, how that Christ died for our sins according to the scriptures. (1 Cor. 15:3)

3. To show people their transgressions.

    Cry aloud, spare not, lift up your voice like a trumpet, and shew my people their transgression, and the house of Jacob their sins. (Isa. 58:1)

4. Preach the news of salvation in Jesus.

    Go ye into all the world and preach the gospel to every creature. (Mark 16:15)

5. We preach that anybody that believe in Jesus can have eternal life.

    For God so loved the world that he gave his only begotten son, that whosoever believeth in him should not perish, but have everlasting life. (John 3:16)

6. We teach the resurrection from the dead.

    Being grieved that they taught the people and preached through Jesus the resurrection from the dead. (Act 4:2b)

7. We preach Jesus Christ.

    And daily in the temple and in every house, they ceased not to teach and preach Jesus Christ.

8. That Jesus came to save sinners.

    This is a faithful saying and worthy of al acceptation, that Christ Jesus came into the world to save sinner. (1 Tim. 1:15)

9. We testify that God the Father sent Son to be our Savior.

    And we have seen and do testify that the father sent his son to be savior of the world. (1 John 4:14)

10. That Jesus died, was buried, and rose again.

    And that he was buried and that he rose again the third day according to the scriptures. (1 Cor. 15:4)

11. We preach that the faith we are overcomers.

    And this is the victory that overcometh the world, even our faith. (1 John 5:4b)

12. If we believe that Jesus is the Son of God, we are overcomers.

    Who is he that overcometh the world but he that believeth that Jesus is the son of God. (1 John 5:5)

WHAT GODS SHOULD AVOID AT ALL TIMES

God is holy and cannot behold iniquity. We must be holy, for God is holy.

1. Pride.

   Not a Novice, lest being lifted with pride he fall into condemnation of the devil. (1 Tim. 3:6)

2. Avoid being ignorant of the devices of Satan.

   Lest Satan should get an advantage of us for we are not ignorant of his devices. (2 Cor. 2:11)

3. Avoid sin: sin is any want of conformity to or transgression against God and His law.

   For all have sinned and come short of the glory of God. (Rom. 3:23)

   Also, **The wages of sin is death.** (Rom. 6:23)

4. Speak no wrong things.

   The lips of the righteous know what acceptable. (Prov. 10:32A)

5. A void anger—infuriate, annoy, irritate, enrage There are different kinds of anger, namely,

   (1) explosive, (2) passive, (3) sarcasm, and (4) depression.

   The result of unresolved anger always leaves the person sick and needing help.

6.   Avoid doubt.

Jesus answered and said unto him; ''verily I say unto you if ye have faith and doubt, not, ye shall not only do which is done to the fig tree. But also, if ye shall say unto this mountain, be thou removed and be thou cast into the sea.it shall be done. (Matt. 21:21)

But when you doubt,

And immediately Jesus stretched forth his hand… And said "O thou of little faith wherefore didst thou doubt?" (Matt. 14:31)

Doubt rob us of our blessing while faith attract God's gifts and rewards.

7.   Despise not prophesying.

Despise not prophesying. (1 Thess. 5:20)

As gods, we love to prophesy. Thus, saith the Lord and the ministrations of the Holy Spirit of God are needed in our life and in the church.

8.   Depart from evil.

Depart from evil and do good; seek peace and pursue it. (Ps. 34:14)

Another scripture says,

Let love be without dissimulation. Abhor that evil; clear to that which is good. (Rom. 12:9)

9.   Avoid lust.

For all that is in the world, the lust of the flesh, and the lust of the eyes. (1 John 2:16)

Another scripture confirms this:

When goods increase, they are increased that eat them; and what good is there to the owners thereof saving the beholding of them with their eyes. (Eccles. 5:11)

The truth is that most wealth that people crave and acquire kill, and most times accumulates are wasted. Just seeing it grow alone satisfies them. This is vanity.

10.   Avoid faithlessness.

He answereth him and saith, "O faithless generation, how long shall I be with you? How long shall I suffer you?" (Mark 9:19)

Jesus was angry with His disciples when they could not cast out the devil from the boy. They proved to be unteachable, despite all the miracles they witnessed. Today, Jesus will also be disappointed with me and you if we cannot do much exploit despite all we have read and seen. We need to avoid faithlessness.

11.   Avoid any abominable thing.

The sacrifice of the wicked is an abomination unto the lord. (Prov. 15:8)

Another scriptures says:

And there in no wise enter into anything that defileth, neither whatsoever worketh abomination, nor maketh a lie.

12.   Not be ashamed of God.

Be not thou therefore ashamed of the testimony of our lord nor. (2 Tim. 1:8A)

Also,

Yet if any man suffer as Christian, let him not be ashamed,

but let him glorify god on this behalf. (1 Pet. 4:16)

13.   Avoid profanity and vainness.

O Timothy, keep that which avoiding profane and vain babblings and opposition of saena falsely so called. (1 Tim. 6:20)

14.   Avoid foolish questions and genealogies.

But avoid foolish questions and genealogies, and contentions, and strivings about the law. For they are unprofitable and vain. (Titus 3:9)

15.   Avoid being controlled by the belly of appetite.

Whose (god) end is destruction, whose God is their belly and whose glory in their shame, who mind earthly things. (Phil. 3:19)

Many are controlled by their appetite and cravings like money, sex, and food. They are ready to go any length to get money to satisfy that demonic, devilish appetite. Some even kill and refuse to serve the Almighty God today due to this.

16.   Avoid covetousness:

And he said to them "Take heed, and behave of covetousness, for a man life consisteth not in the abundance of the things which he posseseth." (Luke 12:15)

17.   Beware of evil workers:

Beware of dogs, beware of evil workers, and beware of the concision. (Phil. 3:2)

18. Avoid bitterness:

Looking diligently lest any man fool of the grace of God, lest any root of bitterness springing trouble you, and thereby many be defiled. (Heb. 12:15)

19. Let all wrath be avoided:

Let all bitterness, and wrath and anger and clamour, and evil speaking be put away from you will all malice. (Eph. 4:31)

The above scripture also identified

20. Clamor—uproar, vehement continuous yelling, like arguments, should be avoided in the church.

21. Evil speaking—slander and cursing should be avoided.

22. Malice should be avoided. This can be described as "active ill will desire to harm another or to do mischief." Believers should not have malice in his heart against anybody.

23. Avoid being carnally minded.

Because the canal mind is enmity (with) against God, for it is not subject to the law of God, neither indeed can be. (Rom. 8:7)

24. Avoid adultery.

Thou shall not commit adultery. (Exod. 20:14)

25.   Curse not. Avoid cursing.

Bless them which persecute you; Bless and curse not. (Rom. 12:14)

26.   Avoid indecency.

Let all things be done decently and in order. (1 Cor. 14:40)

27.   Don't despise wisdom.

The fear of the lord is the beginning of (wisdom) knowledge, but fools despise wisdom and instruction. (Prov. 1:7)

28.   Avoid all forms of disobedience against God.

For as by one man's disobedience many were made sinners. (Rom. 5:19)

Also in Hebrews 2:2:

For if by the word spoken by angels was steadfast, and every transgression and disobedience received a just recompense of reward.

29.   Avoid a double tongue.

Likewise, must the deacons be grave, not double-tongued.

30.   Do not be double-minded.

A double minded man is unstable in all his ways. (James 1:8)

31.   Avoid drunkenness.

For thieves, nor covetous nor drunkards, nor revilers... Shall inherit the kingdom of God. (1 Cor. 6:10)

32.   Avoid envy:

Charity suffereth long and is kind. Charity envieth not.

Or even envy anybody believer or sinners:

Be thou not envious against evil man, neither desire to be with them. (Prov. 24:1)

33.   Flee youthful attachments and lust.

Flee also youthful lust; but follow righteousness. (2 Tim. 2:22)

34.   Don't grieve the spirit.

And grieve not the holy spirit of God, whereby ye are sealed unto the day of redemption. (Eph. 4:30)

35.   Don't harden your heart when you hear the truth.

Harden not your heart as in the provocation. (Ps. 95:8)

36.   Hate nobody.

He that sayeth he is in the light and hateth his brother, is in darkness even now. (1 John 2:9)

God is love. He loved us so much that He asks us to forgive everyone that trespass against us. So hatred has no basis or excuse to be found in our life. Believers, those who oppress us, and even terrorist who cause us so much pain, God want us to love them and pray for them.

37.   Avoid being judgmental:

Judge not, that ye be not judged. (Matt. 7:1)

38.   Never mock God nor the things of God.

Be not deceived; God is not mocked; for whatsoever a man soweth, that shall he also reap. (Gal. 6:7)

39.   Don't pervert the gospel.

Which is not another; but there be some that trouble you and would pervert the gospel of Christ.

Some Christians try to discourage other believers by bringing up unnecessary issues and strange teachings. This is to distract the minds of the serious and thereby derail their course.

40.   Deny not the power of God.

Having a form of godliness but denying the power thereof, from such turn away. (2 Tim. 3:5)

41.   Don't rob God.

Will a man rob God? Yet ye have robbed me. But ye say, wherever have we robbed thee? In tithes and offerings. (Mal. 3:8)

42.   Sorrow not.

But I would not have to be ignorant, brethren concerning them which are asleep, that ye sorrow not even as others which have not hope. (1 Thess. 4:13)

43.   Fear not at any time. Fear no death.

My heart is sore pained within me: and the terrors of death are fallen upon me. (Ps. 55:4)

Fear brings torment. Cowards die quickly, and faithless people fear death. But the scriptures says,

But God hath not given us the spirit of fear, but of power, and of love, and of a sound mind. (2 Tim. 1:7)

Chapter 2

THE GARDEN OF FALL PROCESS

1.   THE GARDEN EXPERIENCE

Man fell in the Garden of Eden. The fall of man affected the whole mankind.

i.   None were righteous

As it is written there is none righteous, no, not one. (Rom. 3:10)

Another Scripture says,

They are all gone aside, they are all together become filthy: there is none that doeth good, no, not one. (Ps. 14:3)

ii.   How did sin come into the world, we ask?

For as by one man's disobedience many were made sinners. (Rom. 5:19A)

Adam made everybody after him sinners in this world. We all became sinners like Adam and Eve.

iii. Other curses follow due to the sin of Adam and Eve. These are discussed extensively in the beginning chapters.

Chapter 3

The Genesis of the Issue

LIKENESS OF GOD

The likeness of God or attributes of God are all encapsulate in the tree of life, which was in the **garden**. God now put a test or trial before them like he does today.

And the lord God commanded the man, saying of every tree of the garden than mayest freely eat.

But of the tree of the knowledge of good and evil thou shalt not eat of it, for the day that the east thereof thou shall surely die. (Gen. 2:16–17)

Remember that man is still in the process of completion, i.e., created in Gods image but not yet his likeness.

<u>WHY?</u>

1.   The likeness of God Jesus Christ

2.   The likeness of God cannot sin

3.   Cannot fall

4.   Cannot be deceived

5.   Is excellent and discipline

6.   Likeness of God

7.   Likeness of God in full of the Word and Spirit of God

Adam and Eve were still in their first stages of physical and emotional creation, which can be declared why they have

1.   spirit—certain percentage of God's personality,

2.   soul—intellect, and

3.   body—male and female.

God gave man the freedom to choose of all the tress, meaning different options—either loyalty and rebellion; but they should be ready to free the consequence: death.

Death: severance, expiration, separation.

Despite all these several options, including the tree of life visibly present in the garden, they made a very wrong choice.

And the serpent said unto the woman, ye shall not sure **die**

For God doth know that in the days that ye eat thereof your eyes shall be opened, and ye shall be as gods, knowing good and evil. (Gen. 3:4–5)

This was a contradiction to God's plan of man. God never wanted man to know good and evil. All that God wanted for man was to be like His Son, Jesus, who was present with them in the garden in the form of the tree of life. But they rejected Him and went astray. Had they eaten the fruit from the tree of life, they would have eaten Christ, an embodiment of wisdom, honor, power, wealth, understanding, **house,** etc. Rather, they chose to believe the serpent instead of God.

And when the woman saw that, the tree was good for food, and that it was pleasant to the eyes, and a tree to be deserved to make one wise, she took of the fruit thereof, and did eat, and gave also unto her husband with her and did eat. (Gen. 3:6)

This was the beginning of Adam's calamity in life. The first man had been tempted and fallen for a very simple strategy of Satan:

1. The loss of the flesh

2. The loss of the eye

3. The pride of life

Imitating is the fact that

1. the process of making is yet to be completed;

2. the process of making has now been stalled by their mistake or action; and

3. they have put mankind into very **service**, spiritual, **mental**, emotional perch logical, and even physical problem, **hereby finance**.

Because of their fall, they became afraid of God—the same God that created them and loved them.

And the lord God called unto Adam, and said unto him, where at thou?

And he said, I heard your voice in the garden, and I was afraid, because I was naked. (Gen. 3:9–10)

I really feel for Adam and Eve, because I cannot imagine the trauma after **severance** from God, the spirit of joy and peace. Jesus experienced it on the cross and cried out, "ELI, ELI Lamasabatani?" (Lord **have**, why hath thou forsaken me?).

I do not want this book to become another book that **enters** eschatology, but I would like to compare this situation to what Christians, unbelievers, and even Jesus faced on daily basis—pain, anguish, and a vacuum that only God created and that only God can fill.

CONSEQUENCES OF THEIR UNBELIEF

1.   Man became naked and ashamed and vulnerable.

2.   The serpent came unto a severed curse.

3.   The woman was cursed severely.

4.   Adam also came under a very serious curse.

All these curses did not end with Adam and Eve alone, but across from generation to generation until Jesus came:

And the lord God said, behold man is become as one of us, to know, good and evil: and now, lest he put forth his hand and take also of the tree of life and eat, and live forever. (Gen. 3:22)

God never wanted man to be like the devil or Satan, who has knowledge of God at a time and walked with God. Ezekiel 37: "but **host** it when he rebelled against God and lost his place."

At last, God declared,

So, he adore out the man and placed at the east of the Garden of Eden cherubim's a flaming sword which tunnel in every way to keep the way of the tree of life. (Gen. 3:24)

Man was banished from the garden, the process of completely making man into the likeness of God became incomplete and therefore postponed till Jesus came.

And I will put enmity between they and the woman, the between thy seed and her seed, It shall bruise thy head and thou shall bruise his heel. (Gen. 3:15)

He calleth them gods unto whom the Word of God has come to and the scripture cannot be broken. (Amos 3:3)

These words were said by our Lord Jesus Christ. He was answering to different accusation from oppositions who claimed he was blasphemous, rude, and utterly out of order. Sometimes in life, when we try to take a stand and become exactly who and what God wants us to become, the accusers, in form of reputable and even the masses, oppose us more. Jesus quoted Psalm 82:6:

He, I have said that ye are gods, and all of you are children of the most high.

The key points in the above passage says the following:

1.   He (God) called them (people, Israelites) gods.

2.   Unto whom the word came to—the word is the testimony of God. The word is also the following:

   (1) the life of God,

   (2) the light of God unto our path,

   (3) the lamb of God to our feet,

   (4) the Word of God is God,

   (5) the Logos,

   (6) and the Rhema—the spirit of God.

3.   The scripture cannot be broken.

   This tells us that what God had said is final in regard to our reputation as gods.

The decision to make men and woman who receive Jesus, the Word of God into their life, is final; and that the decision automatically makes them or transforms them into gods, exactly the image and likeness of God.

TRANSFORM FROM MEN TO GOD

When men received Jesus as their Lord and Savior, there are so many changes that occur. Transformation is defined as (1) to change the form or outward appearance, (2) to change the form condition or function (form), and (3) to change the personality and character of something. This could affect the entire composition of it. Basically, a new person, place or thing.

1.   They become curious of God.

    In the beginning was the word, and the word was with God, And the word was God. He was in the beginning with (him) God all things were made by him without him was not anything made that was made. In him was life and the life was the light of men. (John 1:1–4)

    Jesus satisfied another man's curiosity when He said,

    I am the way and the truth, and the life, No one comes to the father except through me. (John 14:6)

    Have Jesus lay to rest every doubt and every curiosity about who His person is.

2.   They begin to seek wisdom.

    If any of you lacks wisdom let him ask God, who gives generously to all without reproach, and will be given him. (James 1:5)

    When people become transformed to the likeness of God, they begin to enjoy the wisdom of God. They see the fickleness of man and depravity of the world. Something in them begin to seek a higher power. A higher **dominion** of living, better than this modern world. They began to seek the wisdom of God. Wisdom, the Bible says, is the principal thing in life.

    Wisdom is the principal thing. (Prov. 4:7)

Wisdom is so important that the scripture says,

Through wisdom is a house built.

By wisdom, we built everything in life. By wisdom, God created all things, so we need wisdom to succeed in our career, marriage, business, sports, schools, etc.

TWO TYPES OF WISDOM

1.   Wisdom of the world

2.   Wisdom of God

The wisdom of this world: This is the wisdom that the scripture referred to as temporary, unclean, and unacceptable to God. This kind of wisdom is contrary to the word and the way of God. It is not recommended for use by the children of God. This kind of wisdom is from the devil.

ABUNDANT LIFE—God promised all His children abundant life:

The thief comes only to steal and kill and destroy. I came that they may have life and have it abundantly. (John 10:10)

This verse explained God's good intention of abundance, opulence, and more than enough for those who believe him. God created man to enjoy life and not to endure life—scarcity, poverty, lack, and penury. The thief's (Satan) agenda from the beginning is to steal man's joy and replace it with pain, anguish, and suffering. He is a liar. Right from the beginning, Jesus proclaimed,

He is the father of liars because he too was a liar from beginning. (John 8:44)

Jesus further declared,

The spirit of the lord God is upon me, because he was anointed to proclaim good news to the poor. He has sent me to proclaim liberty to the captures and recovering of sight to the blind to set liberty those who are oppressed. (Luke 4:8)

Jesus told them of the prophecy they already know and made them understand that the prophecy is being fulfilled today.

And he began to say to them today the scripture has been fulfilled in your hearing. (John 4:21)

Huge bills to pay, enemies at the gate, **mental** issues, children out of control, etc. So many things to take care of, but very little one can do without God today.

Like David, the voice of that shepherd boy is still ringing out to us today in the twenty-first century. David knew all the battles he won were by the grace of God. He became kind over Israel by his grace. He further declared,

For he will deliver you from the snare of fowler and the deadly pestilence.

Deadly situations, combat, hidden agenda of unscrupulous elements, gang-up and family disputes, witchcraft, office politics, and satanic traps and stubborn pursuers.

In Psalm 91:4, He says **"He will cover you with his pinons and under his wings you will find refuge. His faithfulness is a shield and buckler."**

So also, you—that man or woman, boy or girl, teenagers and children— reading this book, take it that this scripture is also fulfilled in your hearing, in Jesus's name. Amen.

Jesus promise of abundant life is still available today. Go for it by giving your entire life, family, and business to Him; and see God's perspective of abundance against stealing, malpractice in business, drug sales and peddling, prostitution, stealing, robbing, and killing people to get rich. All these will lead one to perdition and eternal damnation. But the **"glory of the lord maketh rich and does not add sorrow to it."**

Jesus is anointed to make people rich. To proclaim good news to the poor. The poor are those who have come to their (1) **witsened**; (2) those who know they are empty without Jesus: "**Without me you can do nothing**"; (3) those who depend on the lord, for their daily bread: "**Give us this day our daily bread**" (Matt. 6:11); (4) those who follow and do only the will of God: "**Nevertheless not my will but you will be done**"; and (5) people who rest on the Lord.

Shadow by the reflection of light. The following verse of Psalm 91:2 explains this:

I will say of the lord my refuge and my fortress, my God in whom I trust.

When David faced the enemies of Jehovah, his enemies, and the enemies of Israel, he noticed the victory he won by the hand of Jehovah.

David saw the grace of the Almighty God amidst his **afraid** self, the outside enemies, and the enemies on the side. He declared somewhere, "The battle is the lord."

He, David, went on and on in verse 3.

"**For he will deliver you from the snare of the fowler and from the noisesome pestilence**" (Ps. 91:3). Too many noise today, family noise.

"**Jesus answered them, is it not written in your law, I said, ye are gods**" (John 10:34). Jesus was answering a group of people who wanted to stone him.

"**Then the Jews took up stones again to stone him**" (John 10:31). Jesus was caught in a very frustrating situation here. He was trying to explain deep things about the messiah and the messianic evidence or proofs already manifest, but they were blind, too blind to see. They accused him of blasphemy:

The Jews answered him, saying for a good work we stone thee not; But for blasphemy and because that thou being a man, makest they self-God. (John 10:30)

Does this sound like the same thing going on in your mind right now? Are you already doubting if God actually said that and why Jesus referred it? Nothing to worry about it; Jesus was just quoting Psalm 82:6:

I have said, ye are.

God is the same, yesterday, today, and forever. He has not gone back on what He said through David's psalms. No wonder Jesus confidently quoted that scripture just to remind His distractors what was already written in the scripture. Some theologians reading this book may soon become convinced about the good intentions of God in bringing man to His level of mind and thinking.

Key features of that verse exposed the fact that He (God) called mankind gods.

WHY DID HE CALL MANKIND gods? Most times, God will use name-calling or name charge as a tool to jolt man out of spiritual stupor or inertia.

1.   Name change as (Abraham's example):

Neither shall thy name anymore be called Abram, but thy name shall be Abraham, for a father of many nations have I made thee. (Gen. 17:5)

Abram means childless, but Abraham—father of plenty or many nations.

2.   2. Simon (Peter) example:

Thou art Simon the son of Jona, thou shalt be called Cephas which is by interpretation A Stone. (John 1:42)

Simon means a shaky reed. Cephas or Peter—a stone.

3. SERAH'S EXAMPLE:

And God said unto Abraham, as for sa-rai thy wife, thou shall not call her name se-rai, but Sarah shall her name be. (Gen. 17:16)

Serai means barren, childless; Serah implies this:

And I will bless her and give thee a son also of her, ye I will bless her, and she shall be a mother of nations; Kings of people shall be of her. (Gen. 17:16)

God gets to us by bringing us to his level of thinking so He can bless us. You cannot walk with God unless you understand Him.

Then opened he their understanding, that they might understand the scriptures. (Luke 24:45)

When thought is open, the light of gospel can penetrate, and this is a blessing.

WHY DO WE NEED UNDERSTANDING OR KNOWLEDGE?

Lack of understanding can make us perish:

For the lord knoweth the way of the righteous, but the way of the ungodly shall perish. (Ps. 1:6)

Knowledge and understanding goes together. This could mean infinite of God by which His knowledge of everything in the most perfect manner.

For the lord is a God of Knowledge, and by him actions are weighted. (1 Sam. 2:3b)

GOD CALLS US BY WHAT HE EXPECTS US TO BE

1. Understanding brings (leads to) agreement with God.

   Can two walk together, except they be agreed. (Amos 3:3)

It is impossible to benefit from God anything without coming to terms with His own ways and life. To me, this is only possible through Jesus Christ.

For there is one God and one mediator between God and men, the man Christ Jesus. (1 Tim. 2:5)

God is our creator and our maker. I personally see creation to be a short-term thing. But making involves a long process, painstaking, and very tedious to a chime. Both words sometimes used interchangeably: Nevertheless, God calls us by

2.   His deposits in us:

And the angels of the lord appeared unto him, and said unto him, the lord is with thee, thou mighty man of valour. (Judg. 6:12)

God sent an angel to Gideon to enlighten him of who he was in the lord. God wants our cooperation with Him at all times and in every situation. He calls us by His own name and sees us through His own strength.

Like most believers (gods), Gideon was shortsighted spiritually and devoid of understanding, hence couldn't properly diagnose the angelic visitation Gideon answered, thus,

Gideon said unto him oh my (God) lord, if the lord be with us? Why then is all this befallen us? And where be all his miracles which our fathers told us of saying. (Judg. 6:13A)

To Gideon, and too many believers today, the journey of life in Christ Jesus is perceived to be a bed of roses only. Anytime we experience trials and challenges along the way, we cry wolf— oh, it is time to complain, murmur, and even backslide. No, the kingdom journey is not a bed of roses only; but persecution, trials, and temptation is part of the packaged.so sit up.

GOD CALLS US GOD BECAUSE OF THE WORD WE RECEIVED

1. He called them gods as a reminded of who they ought to be.

    I have said ye are gods, and all of you are children of the most high. (Ps. 82:6)

    In the context of this particular verse, the children of Israel were reminded of their proper disposition. Like us today, they were peculiar people, sons of God, and needed to focus on that. But anything otherwise will lead to tragedy; verse 7 explains the consequence of shift:

    But ye shall die like men, fall like one of the princes. (Ps. 82:7)

    God is speaking to us that we are not ordinary men and therefore should not behave like one. We are peculiar people in God through Christ. We are God's image and therefore need to behave as such.

    But ye shall die like men.

    Only men die. Gods don't die ordinary death; gods like Christ ascend into heaven, and they go like Elijah. They are more like Samson—very powerful. They are mighty like David and rich like Abraham, Isaac, and Jacob.

    They are rulers like Joseph, conquers like Moses, and dominate heaven and earth like Jesus. They subdue princes and nations. They are like God, lions who don't harm **everything** or are afraid. They are mighty because their Father is the mighty.

    He calls us God to WHOM HAD RECEIVED HIS WORD.

    If he called them gods, unto whom the Word of God came, and the scripture cannot be broken. (John 10:34)

    Those who receives the Word of God into their hearts become gods. They embrace his word and act on the word. They produce the exact thing they will of God. An example is Mary:

And Mary said, behold the handmaid of the lord; be it unto me according to the word. And the angel departed from her. (Luke 1:38)

Mary took in as soon as she accepted the commitment from God. When we accept the Word of God, it produces so many things. It changes the following.

Chapter 4

ACCEPTING THE COMMITMENT

WHAT THE WORD DOES.

1.   It changes our perspective in life.

2.   It is not the word of men, so therefore must be taken seriously.

Ye received it not as the words of men, but as it is in truth, the Word of God. (1 Thess. 2:13)

3.   The word when received can cause problems in manage business, office, etc.

The Joseph her Husband being a just man, and not willing to make her a public example was minded to put her away privily. (Matt. 1:19)

Joseph here was planning to annul the engagement between himself and Mary. He knows the consequences of a public show. Many would have been stoned to death. Killed by a mob, as the scripture or the law said. But many took the risk of rather obeying God or man. What was Mary thinking when she accepted the will of God?

Risks, risks, and many risks are involved in the race to success in the kingdom. Joseph considered the implication of losing his lovely girlfriend. But God had to intervene. Oh, oh. "**God**

will not leave you comfortless." Every day at work, home, park, cinema, public places Christianity is proclaiming Christ is becoming very, very risky. We need the boldness of God to help us to stand and defend our freedom.

Freedom to associate, express ourselves, and proclaim Christ. The Spirit of Christ has been speaking to rulers, government officials and others about us. Therefore, fear not. God will speak to the ruler's wives and children on your behalf. See example:

PILATE'S WIFE'S EXPERIENCE

When he was set down on the judgment seat, his wife sent unto him saying, Have thou nothing to do with that just man, for I have suffered many things this day in a dream because of him. (Matt. 27:19)

God had to speak to Pilate's wife through a dream. She confessed of much trouble in her dream and sought to release Jesus. But what is written is written. When we go through many diverse temptations, know that God is at work in us and will not forsake us in it.

But the chief priest and elders persuaded the multitude that they should ask Banabbas and destroy Jesus. (Matt. 27:30)

JESUS'S EXPERIENCE

1.   He was accused.

And when he was accused of the chief priest and elders, he answered nothing. (Matt. 27:12)

Jesus didn't defend himself. Because if He had, He would have been set free. But the specific instruction of the word, He must have received from the Father is "shut up and say how did you know Okon, I will answer because of his action." He said nothing, and even Pilate complained.

The Pilate said unto him hearest thou not how many things witness against thee. And he answered him to never a word;

in so much that the governor marveled greatly. (Matt. 27:13–14)

Every accused person in a fair trial needed an attorney or is accorded the right or privileged to defend himself. In this particular incident, because of you and I, Jesus decided to keep quiet. He was prepared to die for us and pay the ultimate price, which is death. Jesus loves us and kept His goal. Pilate was seeking an opportunity for Him to defend Himself, so he, Pilate, could release Jesus. Remember, Pilate became governor because of his marriage to Caesar's cousin. The wife was actually ruler of Israel. But the plan to release Jesus became complicated when He refused to speak and defend the allegations against Him. Wow.

SONS OF GOD ARE GODS

SONS—Usually used for male offspring of both parents. Descendant of a parent.

1.   The word *sons* can also be used to explain both female and male gender of God's children. Example:

But as many as received him, to them gave the power to become the sons of God, even to them that believe on his name. (John 1:12)

In this passage, *son* is used. For everybody who cares to believe in the son of God, Jesus. So we too shall try to eliminate strict gender usage of male and female or limit ourselves to this board use, but rather look at the spiritual benefit of the topics examined.

SONS here could also mean offspring.

Offspring—child, progeny, issue, descendant, and heir.

The descendants of a man and woman, most times, carry

striking similarities with parents of the object in question, be it human being, animals, plants, insects, etc.

This resemblance will be both physical, emotional, DNA, certain traits that are peculiar to that family like scars; dentition; steps; occupation; blood group; what they like—including food, women they love, and places they choose; habits; and hobbies—golf, hockey, soccer, football, etc.

These and other traits—whether cultural value, traditions, environment, and attitude or disposition—affect the way people behave and relate with others.

JESUS, THE SON OF GOD

This is a title of Christ that emphasizes His deity and right to the throne of God. An angel met Mary and told her she would give birth to the Son of God:

And the angel answered and said unto her, the Holy Ghost shall come upon thee, and the power of the highest shall over shadow; therefore that holy thing which shall be born of thee shall be called the son of God. (Luke 1:35)

Perfect. Jesus's birth was revealed by the angel to Mary. He will be conceived a baby and will grow up like a normal child, till He is of age to do the work of the Father.

And Jesus increased in wisdom and stature, and in favour with God and with man. (Luke 2:52)

This tells us of His obedience to God, His conduct within the community, and His demeanor in the synagogue. Jesus was scoring points in the kingdom. He grew in wisdom—studied scriptures, prayed, and attended synagogue activities. He grew in stature, into a full-grown man without sin, drugs, women, sex, alcoholism, and other activities typical of his age or peer group. Jesus was not distracted by the vices of His time and therefore quickly earned for Himself a reputation as Son of God. We learn to imitate this noble character of Jesus.

A voice from heaven came after Jesus was baptized; a voice from heaven roared and declared with force so that everybody heard it like a Sinai experience:

And lo a voice from heaven, saying, this is my beloved son, in whom I am well pleased. (Matt. 3:17)

The voice from heaven was a confirmation of the secret life of Jesus publicly. Jesus lived a perfect life, both in secret and in public. He also ensured that what He did was according to the will of God.

But John forbad him saying, I have need to be baptized of thee, and comest thou to me? And Jesus answering said unto him. 'Suffer it to be so now: for thus it becometh us to fulfill all righteousness.' Then he suffered him. (Matt. 3:14–15)

Jesus was not a proud man. He's priority was to obey God and obey Him in totality and wholeheartedly. Despite John the Baptist's somewhat correct appraisal of the time. Jesus knew He was wrong. When it comes to God, obedience must be 100 percent and nothing less. Ninety-five percent obedience and 5 percent disobedience is still disobedience. Be warned. Until He got out of that water, nothing happened. But immediately, Jesus complied with the term of the Father. Then the Holy Spirit came:

And Jesus when he was baptized went up straightened out of the water; and lo, the heavens were opened unto him, and he saw the spirit of God descending like a dove, and lighting upon him. (Matt. 3:16)

Jesus is our perfect example. He knew that obedience to God's word must not be compromised or taken in vain. Even unto death, Jesus was obedient. The passage told us the following:

1.   The heavens were opened unto Him

2.   He saw the Spirit of God descending upon Him.

3.   A voice from heaven was saying, "This is my beloved son in whom I am well pleased."

God is pleased with Jesus. He will be pleased with us too if we recognized who we are in Christ Jesus and gout messing around like ordinary man. As sons of God, as gods, the stake is high for us. The huddle is lifted, and that is the reason "judgment will start from the church." The question once asked by me was, Is this possible today?

After over thirty years of ministry and work in the Lord as an evangelist and pastor, I have come to Jesus that it is impossible with man.

For with God nothing shall be impossible. (Luke 1:37)

GOD AND GODS (MEN) UNITED

UNITED OF THE gods (believers)

UNITY—union, harmony, agreement, concert, unison, rapport, congruity, or concord.

UNITY can be defined as (1) the state of being one or united, oneness, singleness; (2) something complete in itself; (3) the act of being one in the spirit, sentiment purpose, etc., harmony, uniformity; and (4) the quality of fact being a totality of whole especially a complex that is a union or related part.

GOD'S UNITY IN HIMSELF

A perfect example of unity is found in God Almighty.

1.   JESUS AS ONE WITH THE FATHER

My father which gave them to me is greater than all, and no man is able to pluck them out of my father's hand.

I and my Father are one. (John 10:29–30)

The above scripture enlightens us on the closure that exist between God the Father and the Son. The united is so strong that Jesus boldly declared, "We are one." We can be boldly say the same thing. Yes, we can if we put our total trust in God like Jesus, our model, did. He gave all to the Father. The question is, Could this be Jesus's secret for omnipotent power? Yes, is the answer. Jesus didn't even disobey or shy away from the instruction of God because of death. He boldly declared,

Nevertheless not my will but your will be done.

Wow. The second question is this, could our secret to omnipotence be Christ Jesus? Jesus declared in Revelation 12:11:

And they overcome him by the blood of the lamb, and by the word of their testimony; and they loved not their lives unto death.

It is blood for blood declared that scripture, our overcoming the enemy is by the blood of Jesus, the Lamb of God and the word—testimony of our faith. And the second part (B), "And they didn't love their lives even unto death." This is not popular among present-day believers. Present-day believers must see the reality of the (B) part of that verse.

Gods ARE NOT AFRAID OF DEATH.

1.   Death has no power over believers again.

2.   Death is defeated.

3.   Death is a necessary pre-requisite and the fear of it is considered cowardly by God.

We shall look more of that in subsequent passage.

2.   THE FATHER IN CHRIST JESUS

Believe the works, that ye may know, and believe that the father is in me and I in Him. (John 10:38)

Jesus declared, "The Father is in me, that is the reason you see all the good work I do." Miracles and signs are evidences that God is united with us, because He is the one doing the wonders and the miracles. Not fake miracles, but genuine healing, sign, wonders, and other good works. Whoever is in God's agenda and in oneness will bear the fruits of righteousness and does it is confirm by signs and wonders.

3.   When you see Jesus, you have seen the Father:

Jesus saith unto him. Have I been so long time with you, and yet hast thou not known me, Phillip? He that hath seen me the father, and how sayest thou than, shew us the father? Believest thou not that I am in the father, and the father in me? (John 14:9–10a)

Gods should know better.

1.   As gods we ought to know this. We are no longer ordinary believers. We should more from the elementary doctrines of sprinkling of blood and just acknowledge the word or lip service to greater heights in Christ.

Therefore let us leave the elementary teachings about Christ, and go on to maturity not laying again the foundation of repentance from acts that lead to death and of faith in God. (Heb. 6:1 NIV)

2.   As gods, we should go unto maturity in Christ Jesus. We should not be waiting for instruction when we ought to be instructing others.

Instructions about baptism, the laying of hands, the resurrection of the dead and eternal judgment. (Heb. 6:2)

3.   We should live above the elements of this world. The principle of maturity in Christ Jesus does not permit us again to be yoked with the beggarly elements of the world.

Even so we, when we were children, were in bondage under the elements of the world; but when the fullness of the time was come, God sent forth his son, of a woman, made under the law. (Gal. 4:3–4)

4.   There was once upon a time that were in bondage under the elements of the world, under the shackles of the law—don't eat this, don't do that, etc. But God sent His only Son in the form of a man like us. To do what?

To redeem them that were under the law, that we might receive the adoptions of the sons. (Gal. 4:5)

5.   So we are sons of God. We are children of God. We are offspring of God. We are adopted into the lineage of God through Jesus. We are the same image and likeness with God. Express image of God through Jesus. We should no longer go after the elements of this world but after Jesus.

Beware lets any man spoil you through philosophy and vain deceit, after the traditions of men, after the rudiments of the world and not after Christ. (Col. 2:8)

Beware, the scripture says because they come with sweet words, philosophies, and foolish questions like the devil's "Had God said" kind of questions. Vain philosophies that seem to be true but is not. Be careful who is speaking. Read the Bible yourselves if you can or let somebody read the Bible to you.

6.   As sons, what are we? We are no longer servants; we should no longer behave like ordinary servants with false humility and unmersely fear. We are sons of God:

And because ye are sons, God hath sent forth the spirit of his son into your hearts crying Abba father. (Gal. 4:6)

Because we are sons, God had sent the spirit of His Son into our hearts as a seal of authenticity. We have the spirit of Christ in us. We are authentic, bona fide, original image and likeness of God.

WHAT DOES THIS MEAN?

1.   We are authentic—genuine, real, true.

2.   Original: fundamental.

3.   Bona fide.

4.   Sealed, secured, fixed, firm.

We are gods like God. This is made true if we allow the spirit of Christ dwell in us forever.

TO BE LIKE GOD, YOU MUST DO HIS WILL

The will of God summarizes the entire program and plan for existence. God is the Almighty, the CEO of the big world project; and this reserves the right—and the only right—to reveals his plan or His will.

What then is a will? It is defined as (*a*) a strong and fixed purpose, determination, and (*b*) energy and enthusiasm.

By the "will of God," I mean God's purpose fear everything including existence creation. His determination to see them accomplished is based on his attitude and belief. Strong and fixed are the purpose and plans of God. Therefore, they are very, very reliable, faithful, and good.

As a god, we are expected to have the same nature as our Father, Jehovah God. Jesus came as an expressed image and likeness of God—a perfect example for us who are called to emulate, imitate, and behave like Jesus.

Lions give birth to (cubs) lions, rats give birth to rats, and cockroach gives birth to cockroaches, Then God gives birth to gods:

SEEK HIS WILL ONLY. Not my will but thine be done. (Luke 22:14)

The above scripture explains to us what our attitude and disposition ought to be when faced with a situation—before and during a crisis situation, school or academic future, marriage, and even every life endeavors. We should seek to do His will, and only His will shall be done. God will give us direction. Jesus, our perfect model, has this to say:

I seek not mine own will, but the will of the father. (John 5:30b)

Jesus is still the most successful personality in the whole world. This statement, along with others, give us an insight to His secret; Jesus said He sought to do only the will of the Father and not His. Wow. Today, we ought to learn a lesson from our Savior, Jesus.

To be like God, you must trust Him.

1.   A firm belief or confidence in honesty, integrity, reliability, justice, fairness, etc. of another person or person or thing; faith reliance.

2.   Confident expectation, anticipation to the fact of having confidence placed on something.

Our trust should be on God's ability, nature, and law. The world is full of liars today. Trust is a very scarce virtue in the twenty-first-century world. Little or no trust exist again among families, government, politicians, children, and even society. The church that hitherto was the holy place of trust now, and one needs to look closely and be smart not to be duped (sorry to say this).

The Lord remains the only hope of the entire mankind:

Commit thy way unto the lord; trust also in him. (Ps. 37:5)

David discovered the secret about God. No wonder he won all the battles.

Solomon, his son, the wisest man that ever lived in his own time, also had this to say:

Trust in the lord with all your heart and learn not on your own understanding. In all your ways acknowledge him and he shall direct your path. (Prov. 3:5–6)

Man today has many challenges and issues that need answers. Some cases need twenty-four-hour answers, immediate answers, and long-term response. In all these different instances and scenario, the trust of family members, coworkers, and even friends on us to make the right decisions depend on God. Trusting in the power of God's judgment most time even all the time lead us to success.

"Learn not on your own understanding," it says, because man's understanding is limited. For example, there was the case of a man wanted to start a business. He needed to know the business start. This man was an engineer by profession. Beginning to consult with his mind and his friends, he decided to do a business around engineering, which appears to be his comfort zone. Off course, he can go into construction, building or electrical, car manufacture, etc.; but when he sought the face of the Lord, God gave him a very different answer. He was told to do a real estate job. When he obeyed God, this man, today, is happy and rich.

Trusting in the will of God makes our face to shine. We excel in the things we do and therefore become good example to others in the faith.

The question we have now is this:

<u>HOW DO I KNOW GOD'S WILL?</u>

As the image and likeness of God, knowing God's will certainly helps knowing the will of God will align us into His pathway for success. A few guides to this truth includes the following:

1.   HOLY SPIRIT GUIDE OR PROMPTING

       The spirit shall guide you unto howbeit when he, the spirit of truth, is come he will guide you into all truth. (John 16:13)

The Holy Spirit is the spirit of truth. He does guide people all the time. All the patriarchs in the Bible and Christian today who have excelled in career and ministry all own their exploits to the leading and loving guidance of the Holy Spirit. Even I, the writer of this book, can give you numerous circumstances and situations that the Holy Spirit became the only saving grace.

REAL-LIFE TESTIMONY

One day back in Lagos, Nigeria, I was seriously broke and in need of some money. I felt the Holy Spirit was leading me to go to a certain road and wait there. Precisely at Western Avenue Road, I obeyed and stood on that road for some time, although can't tell how long. After a while, I decided this was it; I was not going to stand any longer. While I was about to leave that spot, I had a sister (Rose) called me. She was in a car, and she beckoned on me to get into the car. After settling in the car, she asked, "Why you were standing on that spot like that alone?" I answered, "I don't know, but the Lord asked me to." She then said I was weird and that I kept acting weird all the time. Later that day, she gave me some money to take care of myself.

All the time, God leading makes us weird or help us to look crazy. This is because the Holy Spirit reveals to us the truth about God's love for us.

For God so love the World. (John 3:16)

This is in direct contrast to what the enemy Satan wants the world to believe. The devil has filled mankind or humanity with the wrong ideas that "God hates mankind so much." He keeps bombarding the people of the world with wrong information about who they are. So the Holy Spirit, which is the spirit of truth, leads and guides us to know who we really are in Christ Jesus—the benefit of our sonship in Jesus. Jesus relied totally 100 percent, if you like, on the guide and prompting of the Holy Spirit. He never started His ministry until the Holy Spirit came upon after baptism of John.

Read this:

And Jesus being full of the Holy Spirit returned from Jordan, and was led by the spirit into the wilderness. (Luke 4:1)

The people that are led by the spirit of God do the right thing always. This is because the Holy Spirit is an excellent spirit.

People that a led by the spirit of God are sons of God.

Another scriptures says,

The things of God knoweth no man, but the spirit of God. (1 Cor. 2:11)

Where do gods look for God's will? The children of men look for the will of their father in his closet or the attorney's chamber. The first place to look for God's documented will—Logos—is in his word. These words have been written down for thousands of years in the Bible.

THE BIBLE—The Bible is God's written records of His revelations. This is accepted by Christians all over the world as uniquely inspired and authoritative for faith practice. God inspired the writing of the Bible over one thousand years ago, from the time of Moses through the first century AD. The New Testament and the old books, or Old Testament, make up what we call the Bible today. This book contains both direct verbatim instruction and speech of God and also eye-witness accounts of events and statements made by God, His prophets, and His teachers of the world of God. The Bible is unique and authentic, tested and certified truth because men were moved by the Holy Spirit and inspired to write down these words.

All scripture is given by the inspiration of God, and it is profitable for doctrine, for reproof, for correction, for instruction in righteousness. (2 Tim. 3:16)

The question now is, Why was the scripture given to us? We find the answer in the next verse:

That the man of man be perfect, thoroughly furnished unto all good works. (2 Tim. 3:17)

The Word of God contains the life, instruction, will, and rewards of god. So God took time to have this word documented and preserved for thousands of years. Therefore, adequate information about the role of God and the role of gods (man of God) are clearly enshrined.

ONLY THOSE THAT RECEIVED HIS WORD ARE CALLED GODS

Jesus said, **(And) if he called them gods unto whom the Word of God came, and the scripture cannot be broken.** (John 10:35)

Sons of God go into the scriptures to look at themselves. They see who they are when they see who God's Son is: All-powerful, wonderful, counselor, mighty God. He is the Word of God. So also we should conform into the will of God and be little gods. Not like idols of Satan or idols of evil, like the world knows it to be. But rather idols of righteousness, icons on earth. People who walk like Him and do everything like God. Gods (man) sanctified by the Word of God (Jesus) must commune with the Almighty God. The communication must be through the word (Holy Spirit). Gods must be operated by the Holy Spirit before they can function as gods. Gods must dive deeper into the world of the holy truth, which is only revealed by the spirit of God Himself.

Gods must remain with their Father, Jehovah God, at all times; gods must eat what God eats.

There is a food I eat that none of you know about.

Another translation says,

I have meat to eat that ye know not off. (John 4:32)

Gods must understand God. Deep call unto the deep. There are deeper things God Almighty, Jesus, and the Holy Spirit are sharing with us on a daily basis, per –per second that ordinary Christian cannot understand, talk less of ordinary people. The Word of God is not philosophy.

PHILOSOPHY—From the Greek word **EAOC**, meaning "a lover audial wisdom." In Colossians 2:8, Apostle Paul warned the Colossians about the trap of philosophy:

Beware lest any man spoil you through, philosophy and vain deceit, after tradition of men, after the rudiments of thing world, and not after Christ.

Most people fall for traps like this, and eventually lose their conviction, and their faith becomes bankrupt. Understand, Apostle Paul bid the Colossians beware—i.e., take heed, be careful, or watch out. Luke related that when Paul came to Athens, he found Epicurean and stoic philosophers who mock his conversation or discourse on the way of the cross. Those philosophers have some influence on the people that their tradition was more of man—vain, deceitful, and of worldly pleasures— that they were not interested in the providence of God.

Then certain philosophers of the Epicureans and stoics encountered him. And some, what will this babbler say? Other some. He seemeth to be a setter forth of strange gods; because he preach unto them. Jesus and the resurrection. (Acts 17:18)

We are the image and the likeness of God, and we therefore don't believe in the philosophy or wisdom of man. The philosophy of man concentrates on the study of the rudiments or elements of the world, like the sun, moon, earth, water, and also the key operation of scene and wise talks. They have ancient philosophers and kings like Plato, Aristotle, Socrates, etc. These philosophers have written many books and have schools that teach Greek philosophies till death. But compared to the Word of God, which is potent and spirit filled, the answer is no. There is no other name that man can be saved.

The same apostle opposes the false wisdom, and wise man of his age, which was nothing but the pagan philosophy of the devil, always contrary to the wisdom of Christ. He called them more folly, being built neither upon evidence, nor the eloquence and subtlety of the preachers. In today's world, there are so many issues in the church sparkling a lot of controversies. Like the LBTS community, abortion, same-sex marriage, divorce, sex, credit politics, terrorism, etc. All these issues come to the church as well. We have families faced with critical issues that need strong-decision stance. But more than common is the fact that people depend more on how they feel about the issue than what the scripture says. This is especially when family members are involved. Emotions, false love, and hypocrisy—characteristics of today's opinion on very clear stance the holy book took on those issue. These days, people prefer not to talk about it or simply look the other way. Compromise, the philosophy of men are most times contrary to the Word of God and prevail on discussion of politics, TV, family tables, and even offices. No discrimination is allowed.

Discussions on religious matters are forbidden and often criticized, or law suites are arranged. Anonymous law suites attack both open attacks by Christian has become the other of the day.

GOD'S MISSION ON EARTH

As gods, we stand where our Father, Jehovah Elohim, Yahweh, stands. The food of Jesus is the Word of God. His food does the will of God. This is also our meat; it is our life. The will of our Father, God, is also our meat.

It is our meat to do and to finish the work of God. We have the same heartbeat with Jesus.

My meat is to do the will of him that sent. (John 4:34)

Jesus's mission was clear. He job or vocation was to do the will of God. He clearly was focused on doing God's will. Like imitators of Jesus, our model, we need to take cue from the statements. He kept saying everywhere he went that His will was given to Him. Battles irrespective, he kept saying it, living it, and working it. He was a man on a mission. He knew His agenda. He was scheduled to succeed.

We also must know who we are. We must locate who were as earlier discussed and begin to run our course. We are gods on a mission. To think that we are on this earth to live like ordinary man would be foolhardy. To some people, this mission is in a rat circle.

Born—grow up—go to school.

Many raise kids and die, and that's it.

No. Life is more than that to us gods; we need to establish the fact that we are pilgrims on earth.

Pilgrims means foreigner, strangers, people who come from a far place.

These all died in faith, not having, received the promise but having seen them afar off, and were persuaded of them, and embraced them, and confessed that they were strangers and pilgrims on the earth. (Heb. 11:13)

As gods, we understand who we are. We know we are from a far place, which is heaven, where God our Father above is. We know we live in holiness; we are sanctified people. We are gods, and we do only what God do. We are going home to the Father whole. On earth, we live in heavenly places. Our light is the Word of God; our lamb is the illumination of the Holy Spirit. Gods don't compromise their grounds. We don't shift places. We are in this world but aren't part of it.

GODS ARE NOT OF THIS WORLD

The world in Hebrew is the **BAL** and is taken to mean the whole wide world—universe, sea, rock, elements, angels, men, women, and also the brain of man that created car, jets, buildings of all shapes, modern world, ancient world, devils, demons, presidents, leaders, and everything creeping or flying. All things are called the world, the operations of this world, etc.

1.   The world has her operations

2.   The values and traditions

3.   Philosophies as discussed earlier, beliefs and systems

4.   Market, laws, and daily activities

All these belong to God Almighty.

The earth is the lords and the fullness thereof; the world and they that dwell therein. (Ps. 24:1)

God founded this present world in holiness and true righteousness. He then gave man authority. But today, the world is corrupt and British. Satan has changed the world order. The earth is out of control. This was why Jesus had to come to set the world back in order and save mankind again. See this statement:

All have sinned and come short of the glory of God.

Man sinned and became short of God's power and privileges. But God Almighty wants us to be not like Satan but like Jesus.

The word *world* could sometimes be used biblically to mean the wicked of this world, the unregenerated or disobedient people.

If the world hate you, ye know that it hated me before it hated you. (John15:18)

We gods love Jesus. We love God, so we are not like the people Jesus referred to at all. Gods love anything that God loves and hate anything God hates. The world hates us because they hate Jesus. The disobedient, the ungodly, can never be comfortable with the righteous; light and darkness can never be together again. God separated them during creation time. "It is good," God declared when He saw it.

Jesus called the wicked the world. The wicked are called the world because they love and devote themselves to enjoy things of this world than the knowledge of God. Hence, Jesus spent His time reconciling the people back to God even unto death.

To wit, that God was in Christ, reconciling the world unto himself not imputing then trespasses unto them and hath committed unto us the word of reconciliation. (2 Cor. 5:19)

As gods, our Father, the king of kings and the god of gods, was inside Jesus, reconciling us to himself. God here reflect the sinners of this world. It means those that have lived in sin and trespasses. We also ought to reconcile sinners to God. We are the priest of God, preachers of Jesus. We are commissioned to tell the good news.

The world also comprises of both Jews and Gentiles alike.

For God so loved the world that he gave his only begotten son; that whosoever believeth in him should not perish but have everlasting life. (John 3:16)

The world we are today is not a place for us to be and forget ourselves. We should be conscious of who we are and where we are going. The worldly system has their own operation, which we don't belong. They even have their own god.

The god of this world had blinded their eyes lest they see the light of the gospel of the glory of Christ. (2 Cor. 4:4)

Here, Satan is called the god of this world. Today there are billions of things created by man and called gods. This sentiment existed long ago and even at the time of Jesus, and afterward, Paul noted this.

Even the Old Testament told us how God felt about idol worship.

They have moved me to jealousy with that which is not God; they have provoked me to anger with their vanities.

As gods or sons of God, we are not expected to worship idols. Idol worship is prohibited. God becomes provoked and jealous when we divert our attention to other grave images. We become filled with vanities—practices, values, and traditions that are strange and alien to the pattern and instruction of God.

He that sacrificeth unto any god, save unto the lord only, he shall be destroyed. (Exod. 22:2)

CONSEQUENCES OF SERVING STRANGE GODS

1.   Destruction—"Every soul that sinneth shall die."

2.   Sorrow multiplied—"Their sorrow shall multiply that hasten after another" (Ps. 16:4).

3.   Rejection of the sacrifices offering—"Their drink offerings of blood will I not offer" (Ps. 16:4b)

4.   Their name became lost—"Nor take up their names into my lips" (Ps. 16:4c)

Have the Lord opens up to us the many consequences of following after strange gods.

Chapter 5

HOW TO TRANSFORM FROM MAN TO GOD

Transform—transfigure, convert, commute alter, change

Transform is defined as (1) to change the form or outward appearance, (2) to change the condition or nature or function of convert or change or convert a voltage, and (3) charge personality.

Man can be described as a human being, as a primate (*Homo sapiens*) having an erect stance, an apposable thumb, articulate speech, and highly developed brain with the faculty of abstract thoughts.

At the beginning of creation, man was created good as the image of God Almighty—the Lord Almighty is perfect and excellent.

Let me remind you again:

So, God created man in his own image in the image of God created he him; male and female created he them. (Gen. 1:27)

This was rather a case of God's protection into the future. This creation was actually done in a future verse. This was fulfilled in Genesis 2:21–25:

And the lord God caused a deep sleep to fall upon Adam; and he slept; and he took one of his ribs, and closed up the flesh instead thereof. And the rib, which the lord God had taken from man, made him a woman. And brought her unto the man.

The likeness of God was projected by God for another day. So far, man was incomplete without God's likeness. But man fell before God's likeness could be implanted or installed in man.

He that is born of God cannot sin; it is impossible for God's likeness to sin. Jesus is our perfect example. Adam and Eve were not yet perfect likeness of God. They may be physical image of God or projected image of a finished protect. But when they tell, they were not yet fully the image and the likeness of God.

Read this:

For whatsoever is born of God overcometh the word. (1 John 5:4A)

The fallen man needs help to get back on course after his fall from grace to grass. Driven out of Eden—the garden of grace to the wilderness, the place of hardship

And unto Adam he (God) said because thou hast hearkened unto the voice of thy wife, and hast eaten of the tree, of which I commanded thee, saying thou shalt not eat of it cursed is the ground for thy sake. It sorrow shalt thou eat of it all the days of the life.

The curses continued into 18 and 19:

Thorns and also thistles shall it bring forth to thee and thou shall eat the herb of the field.

Also; In the sweat of thy shall thou eat bread till thou return unto the ground. For out of it wasn't thou taken; for dust thou art, and unto dust shall thou return. (Gen. 3:17–19)

Man came unto wrath and unto the curse of God. God declared sufferings for both Adam and Eve and, by extension, the entire humanity. Nobody spared. By that curse, the once blessed man became the following:

1.   Cursed man—driven out of God's presence.

2.   The ground was cursed—the yields of the ground were now

filled with thorn and **thistles**.

3.   Man shall eat with sorrow all day.

4.   In his sweet shall man eat ordinary bread.

5.   Man shall become sick, that he will always need the herbs for medicine.

6.   Women shall have sorrowful labor miscarriages, painful menstrual period, and birth complications.

7.   Raising children shall become sorrowful and mind bagging.

8.   Women shall always desire their husband's faithfulness, which will become very scarce; men's unfaithfulness will be very **glaring.**

The world today still shows the presence of all these curses, especially in the homes and lives of both the believers and the ignorant or blind believers. This book I believe will be an eye-opener for those who want to get liberated and receive what Jesus had finished. After the fall of man, God quickly set up a plan of action. He said to the serpent.

And the lord unto the serpent because thou hast done this thou art cursed above. And I will put enmity between thee and the woman, and between thy seed and her seed; it shall bruise thy head, and thou shalt bruise his heel. (Gen. 3:14–15)

This statement set the stage for the coming of our Savior and Messiah, somebody to liberate mankind. Somebody qualified to do this. What was His name? His name was Jesus, the Son of God.

Read this:

TRANSFORMATION THROUGH IMITATING JESUS

For God so loved the world, that he gave his only begotten son, that whosoever believeth in him should not perish but have everlasting life. (John 3:16)

Jesus was sent by the Father to help us regain our lost glory by taking away our sins. Jesus came to be our salvation.

For God sent not his son into the world to condemn the world; but that the world through him might be saved. (John 3:17)

Jesus is that seed of the woman that God spoke about. The seed of the woman that would bruise the head of the serpent.

WHY DID GOD SEND JESUS TO US?

1. To show us His love:

   But commendeth his love toward us, in that while we were yet sinners, Christ died for us. (Rom. 5:8)

2. Through Jesus, we can know and understand God—by imitating Him and becoming like Him.

   Ye neither know me nor my father, if ye had known me, ye should have known my father also. (John 8:19)

   He also proclaimed,

   And Jesus saith unto him have I been so long with you, and lest hast thou not known me Phillip? He that hath seen me hath seen the father. (John 14:9)

3. God sent Jesus to show us exactly what He is like.

   Who is the image of the invisible God, the firstborn of every creature? (Col. 1:15)

   When we imitate Jesus, we will become like the Father that we cannot see. God wants us to get it right. This is because what you focus on for a long time, you become. God wants us to focus on Jesus alone because He alone is the expressed image of the Father.

4. God sent Jesus to show us a perfect example of a good shepherd. We ought to be sacrificial and be ready to give all we are and have to God. God is calling us to emulate and transform into the image of Jesus by giving our life, like Jesus did. Here is the example of the good shepherd:

    I am the good shepherd the good shepherd; the good shepherd giveth his life for the sheep. (John 10:11)

    He also said,

    Greater love hath no man than this, that a may lay down his life for his friend.

5. The death of Jesus paid the debt for our sins. The curses brought death and sorrow through sin. This cannot continue, so God sent His Son to pay the price.

    Christ Jesus came into the world to save sinners. (1 Tim. 1:15)

    Also Jesus said,

    For the son of man is come to seek and to same that which was lost. (Luke 19:10)

    We should imitate and be transformed to Christ's image when we seek sinners wherever we are and give them the message of salvation. There are many, but there those who need to hear this message. The world is hurting and bleeding right now. Be God's messenger to our dying world.

6. We are transformed when we proclaim the truth like Jesus.

    Thou sayeth that I am a king. To this end was I born, kind for this cause came into the world, that I should bear witness unto the truth. Everyone who is of the truth heareth my voice. (John 18:37)

    We bear witness to the truth about salvation. In our personal life, we tell the truth about our salvation. In our personal life, we tell the truth always. The attributes of God will definitely change our perspective of ourselves and keep us closer to God.

7. We transform from man to god when we exercise power over devil. We should destroy their power like Jesus did.

That through death he might destroy him that had the power of death that is the devil. (Heb. 2:14)

Another scriptures reads,

For this purpose was the son, of (man) God was manifested, that he might destroy the works of the devil. (1 John 3:8)

8. Like Jesus, we are transformed into gods when we <u>are</u> touched by the feeling of other people infirmities.

Made like unto his brethren ... in that he himself hath suffered being tempted, He is able to succor them. (Heb. 2:16–18

Jesus had to go through what we go through. He understood us better by humility. He humbled Himself.

9. We become gods through the spirit of humility like Jesus.

Humble thyself (yourselves) therefore under the mighty hand of God, that he may exalt you in due (season) time. (1 Pet. 5:6)

Also

But he gaveth more grace wherefore he saith, the God resisteth the proud, but giveth more grace to the humble. (James 4:6)

10. We transform ourselves and others to become like God when we teach with authority and power.

They were astonished at his doctrine; for his words was with power. (Luke 4:32)

Also spoken of him:

Never man spake like this man. (7:46)

Jesus was operating with power—dunamis and authority

11. We are transformed into image and likeness of God when we receive Jesus as Lord and Savior.

But as many as received him, to them gave the power to become the sons of God, even to them that believe on his name. (John 1:12)

12. We must believe Jesus to be transform into Gods.

Even to them that believe on his name. (John 1:12b)

Believing Jesus makes a big difference. This is because believing Him empowers us.

For him that cometh to God must believe that he is and that he is a rewarder of them that diligently seek him. (Heb. 11:6b)

Sometimes we are tempted to believe God but kind of skeptical of the claims of Jesus. Some say Jesus is like any other prophet, e.g., Muhammad of Islam, Buddha in Buddhism, etc. Today, there are several religions and people claiming to be one thing or some prophets.

Fake Christs, preachers, and prophets emerge from time to time claiming to be capable of doing extraordinary miracles. So far, inconsistences and shocking sexual and demonic scandals mar their trail. This tends to cast aspersion on the institution and the integrity of the church.

As gods or men or women who desire to be perfect, we need

not be discouraged by this scandalous scenarios but forge ahead by believing Jesus.

13.   Believe Jesus no matter what.

Therefore I say unto you what things so ever ye desire when ye pray, believe that ye received them, and ye shall them. (Mark 11:24)

Also the scripture advises:

And whosoever believeth on him shall not be ashamed. (Rom. 9:3)

14.   Gods (believers) obey God. Obedience is very vital, a serious key factor to receiving; God's promotion:

And Samuel said, hath the lord as great delight in burnt offering and sacrifice as in obeying the voice of the lord. (1 Sam. 15:22A)

Men today try to impress God through kind gestures, gifts, and works. This was a case whereby Saul allowed the pressure from the citizens to make him disobey God's instruction. God's instruction was for the king to destroy everything, including humans and beast. But Saul did otherwise. Samuel was so frustrated that he said,

behold, to obey is better than sacrifice, and to hearken than the fat of rams. (1 Sam. 15:22b)

This action cost Saul the throne. He lost the throne through disobedience, the same as Adam and Eve, Samson, Judas Iscariot, etc. Disobedience cause man to lose his authority and power.

For we ourselves also were sometimes foolish, disobedient, deceived.

15.   Gods don't get foolish but wise transformation to gods wonderful icons act wise and make choices.

As gods, we need wisdom:

Wisdom is the principal thing; therefore get wisdom. (Prov. 4:7A)

16.   Gods get understanding.

And with all thy getting get understanding. (Prov. 4:7b)

Wisdom is very good. The Bible says Jesus is the wisdom of God. We need the wisdom from above, which is better and more stable.

But the wisdom that is from above is first pure, them peaceable. (James 3:17A)

What we need is the Jesus wisdom which is from above not the wisdom of the world

For the wisdom of this world is foolishness with God. For it is written, he taketh the wise in their own craftiness. (1 Cor. 3:19)

What the world called wisdom today is more or less foolishness. Foolishness when compared to godly wisdom from above. The secret, sacred wisdom of God is found in the Word of God. The word explains exactly perfect counseling on every issue of life.

Therefore, if anyone needs counsel,

if any of you lack wisdom. Let him ask of God, that giveth to all men liberally and upbraideth not; and it shall be given him. (James 1:5)

Gods ask to receive and not be disappointed.

But let him ask in faith, nothing wavering for he that wavereth is like a wave of the sea driven with the wind and

tossed. (James 1:6)

The gravity of the punishment of Adam and Eve gave us an idea of the depth of God's holiness and intolerance or zero tolerance for sin. Therefore, we need to mobilize every help from God within us, prayer pastor to be able to live right.

ONLY DOERS OF THE WORD ARE GODS NOT doer but only heaven cannot make us transform into gods.

For it any man be a hearer of the word and not a doer, he is like a man beholding his face natural face in a glass. For be beholdeth himself. And goeth his way and straightway forgeteth what manner of man he was Jesus. (James 1:23–24)

Fear of Man

1.   The fear of man robs people of their blessings.

   The fear of man bringeth a snare. (Prov. 29:25)

2.   Fear of church leaders, denominations, and religious affiliations.

Many believed on him, but because of the Pharisees they did not confess him (publicly). (John 12:42–43)

Example is Nicodemus, who came in the night:

There was a man of the Pharisees named Nicodemus a ruler of the Jews the same came to Jesus in the night. (John 3:1–2A)

TRANSFORMATION FROM MAN TO GOD THROUGH PRAYER

PRAYER—appeal, request, petition, plea

Pray—plead, beseech, ask

Prayer is defined as (1) the act of praying to God; (2) an earnest request, entreaty, supplication; (3) a humble and sincere request to God, an utterance to God in praise and thanksgivings, confession, etc.; and (4) could mean a devotional service consisting (consisting) of prayers or any form of communing with God.

God is a model. We do everything to emulate Him. Earlier, we consider Jesus our visible, tangible model. He lived the life and was successful. He therefore recommended it to us.

How to pray: One occasion the followers of Jesus ask for a prayer plan, model, or type like other masters taught their disciples. Then Jesus said,

And he said unto them when ye pray, say our father which art in heaven, Hallowed by thy name. Thy kingdom God, thy will be done, as in heaven.

So in earth, **give us day by day our daily bread And forgive us our sins, for we also forgive everyone that is indebted to us. And lead us not into temptation; but deliver us from evil.** (Luke 11:1–4)

This prayer is very popular among Christians and non-Christians, like Pentecostal, Baptists, Catholics, Lutherans, and every other denominations in the universe. The popular prayer called the Lord's Prayer contains a lot of stuff we need to talk to God about. The disciples asked for this prayer guide or model, if you like, to enhance their prayer life.

Teach us to pray as John also taught his disciple to pray. (Luke 1:1b)

They knew the joy of answered prayer. They know the frustration also of deferred hope and aspiration.

Hope deferred, maketh the heart sick, but when the desire cometh, it is a tree of life. (Prov. 13:12)

So, the disciple's guess for a prayer formula, disciple, or plan was actually in order.

WAYS gods should pray and get transformation or result:

1.   Praise and thank God before petitioning.

   Enter into his gates with thanksgiving, and into his courts with praise; be thankful unto him, and bless his name. (Ps. 100:4)

   The principle of receiving answers to prayer involve us engaging the spirit of thanksgiving at the beginning of prayer and at the middle of it and also at the end.

   Example: Jesus at the tomb of Lazarus.

   So they took away the stone. Then Jesus looked up and said father, thank you that you have heard. I knew that you always hear me. (John 11:41–42b)

   When we thank God at the beginning of our prayer, it shows gratitude confidence in God. The spirit of appreciation triggers the release of answers. This is because the grateful is truthful, and the truthful is grateful, and grateful is prayerful, and the prayerful is hopeful, and the hope becomes fruitful.

   Be careful for nothing; but in everything by prayer and supplication with thanksgiving let your request be made known unto God. (Phil. 4:6)

2.   Pray in tongues; praying like this is good.

   For he that speaketh in an unknown tongue speaketh not unto men, but unto God for no man understandeth him howbeit in the spirit he speaketh mysteries. (1 Cor. 14:2)

   Praying in tongues help us build our fruit and therefore transforms us from ordinary people to wonderful beings.

   Likewise the spirit also helpeth our infirmities; for we know not what we should pray for as we ought; but the spirit itself maketh intercession for us with groaning's which cannot be uttered. (Rom. 8:26)

WHAT DOES PRAYING IN TONGUES DO?

1.   Praying in tongues or in the spirit energizes us.

2.   We speak directly to God and are not distracted by men.

3.   When we pray in tongues, we speak mysteries.

4.   We get help for our infirmities, include inability to diagnose and diagnose

Our problem is to be able to tell God exactly how we feel, but the spirit takes off all the confusion when we pray accordingly.

Hear this:

And he that searcheth the hearts knoweth what is the mind of the spirit, because he maketh intercession for the saints according to the will of God. (Rom. 8:27)

God's plan or blueprint of creation is on-going. He has not abandoned it. The plan of God exists, and man is expected to conform into this plan or blueprint. It takes the creator therefore to effectively complete His work. As a potter, God will endure and finish His creation, and also as a clay, man must be quiet and cooperate with his maker to complete His work.

Hath not the potter power over the clay, of the same lump to make one vessel unto honour and another unto dishonor. (Rom. 9:21)

God controls the universe. He controls the affairs of men. Therefore, a genuine belief that desire transformation from ordinary men to extraordinary people or gods must conform to the likeness of God by submitting themselves to Him through obedience and sufferings.

For I reckon that the suffering of the present time are not worthy to be compared with the glory which shall be revealed in us. (Rom. 8:18)

3. When praying, let us be specific and ask for what we need.

a. "Ask and it shall be given you" (Matt. 7:7A)

b. In our prayer, we need to also "seek and ye shall find."

c. "Knock and it shall be opened" (Matt. 7:7)

Jesus expects us to realize that praying is a serious business. When we bring businesslike approach to prayer, we become very specific.

a. We ask for specific things that we need from God for ourselves, family, friends, nation, church, etc.

b. Our prayer becomes effective and to the point.

c. Our prayers now have direction and can be completed.

d. Our prayer seeks the truth. Through prayer, God opens the realm for deeper answers to hidden questions, therefore allowing us to dive deeper into Him.

e. Prayers help us to specifically knock on the right resources. It gingers us to knock and expect result.

4. Effective prayer must first be asked or prayed in Jesus's name.

If ye ask anything in my name I will do it. (John 14:14)

Also, Jesus declared, **Whatsoever ye shall ask the father, in my name, he will give it you.** (John 16:23)

5. **Prayer of transformation requires you to do the following:**

1. Listen to God always.

Pray:

Therefore Eli said unto Samuel, Go, lie down; and it shall be, if he call thee, that thou shall speak lord for thy servant heareth … And the lord and stood, and called as at other times, Samuel, Samuel, Samuel. Then Samuel answered, speak; for thy servant heareth. (1 Sam. 3:9–10)

2.   Prayer entails meditating.

> **And Isaac went out to meditate in the field at the eventide.** (Gen. 24:63A)

Another scripture says meditation helps to transform us quickly into God's likeness. Deep meditation makes us see a picture of God's nature us and our freckles that need change and transformation. Deep meditation makes us grow into maturity and communion with God.

3.   Our meditation must be in the word, not in world.

> **But his delight is in the law of the lord; and in his law doth he meditate day and night.** (Ps. 1:2)

4.   God gives power to us to become like Him when we pray.

> **He giveth power to the fainted and to them that have no might he increaseth strength.** (Isa. 40:29)

When people become weak and weary due to everyday life activities, they have the option to go to God and spend them in His presence. They need to ask, and they will be given more than enough power to live above the stress of life. No matter how strong we claim or appear to be, sometimes the issues of life keep banging persistently on our doors, and very soon, we must need cry for help from our creator, stress of children, bills, college activities, coworkers, police officers, government officials, legal battles, former employers, ex-lovers, insurance adjustors, healthcare challenges, etc. This daily and weekly everyday activities seem to weigh us down. But when we roll them over to the Lord, He parents us from fainting.

Even the youths shall faint and be weary, and the young men shall utterly fall. (Isa. 40:30)

5.   When we pray, stress is changed to strength. And our weakness is replaced with vigor and vitality.

But they that wait upon the lord shall renew their strength: they shall mount up with wings as eagles: they shall ran and not be weary; and thy shall walk and not faint.

Without God's kind of strength in life, what life throws at us on daily basis is enough to kill even the strongest man in the world. But with God, what appears impossible is done without much stress and hullabaloo. God's strength conveys our little effort and amplifies it to a higher degree that we expected or imagine.

Now unto him that is able to do exceeding abundantly above all that we ask or think according to the power that worketh in us. (Eph. 3:20)

God is able to do more than we anticipate or imagine when we humbly ourselves and pray for his intervention.

MEDITATION

Effective meditation must be on the Word of God and not of the problem. The problem is there, we know, and God is away. But God expects that our focus should be on the solution and not the problem. Our meditation on the word generates.

1.   Hope in God.

2.   Generate faith in the power of God.

3.   It bunds assurance, which in turn encourages the listeners.

4.   Meditation help us to flourish.

And he shall be like a tree planted by the rivers (for water) of water.

5.   Meditation help us to be fruitful in our season.

That brings forth his fruit in his season.

6.   Meditation brings about prosperity.

Whatsoever he doeth shall prosper. (Ps. 1:3b)

Example of Joshua

In Joshua 1:8, God appeared to Moses after the demise of Moses and gave him formally the mandate to take the Israelites to the promise land.

God felt it pertinent to give Joshua his own secret of success. He started by telling him the obvious credentials of Moses, his boss, and secretly told him what he must do to be as successful as Moses his servant.

Now after the death of Moses the servant of the lord it came to pass, that the lord spake unto Joshua the son of Nun, Moses minister saying, Moses my servant is dead; now therefore arise go over this Jordan, and thou and all this people unto the land which do give to them, even to the children of Israel. (Josh. 1:2–3)

Chapter 6

What Gods Should Know and Operate

ANGELS EXISTENCE AND MANIFESTATION

Gods enjoy angelic interactions.

ANGEL: A messenger or bringer of tidings and is those intellectual and immaterial beings whom God made us of as His ministers to execute orders of providence.

And I John saw these things and heard them, and when I had heard and seen, I fell down to worship before the feet of the angel which shewed me these things. (Rev. 22:8)

1.   He shall give His angels to be in charge for us.

     He shall send his angel before thee; and thou shall take a wife unto my son from thence. (Gen. 24:7)

2.   For our redemption.

     The angel which redeemed me from all evil, bless the lads; and let my name be named on them. (Gen. 48:16A)

3.   Angel for our safety and deliverance.

     And when we cried unto the lord, he heard our voice and sent an angel and hath brought us forth out of Egypt. (Num. 20:16)

4. Wondrous performance through the angelic visitation. Angels of God are capable of doing great and wonderful things.

So Manoah took a kid with a meat offering, and offered it upon a rock unto the lord and the angel did wondrously and Manoah and his wife looked. (Judg. 13:19)

DEMONS

People will never be what **and** wants them to be except they did with demons (2 Cor. 10).

We got to get rid of thoughts when bigger demons come in.

DEMON—This is an evil spirit. Evil spirits have destructive tendencies. They possess power opposing God's good intentions.

These evil spirits are capable of cooperating together and have the ability to possess a person and object like trees, houses, rivers, and mountains. This is called evil or demon possession.

Demon possession is the invasion and control of a person by evil spirits.

Possession here could mean to be owned or be controlled by an evil or good spirit, occupy, be crazed, or mad or belonging to.

What do gods do about evil spirit?

The ministry of Jesus is characterized by His dealing with these evil characters called demons.

His healing ministry was a good example for us to understand and emulate.

It is researched and after spoken by scholars that

1. 85 percent of demon-possessed people become critically ill;

2. demons account for basically a large percentage of terminal and incredible discerns today;

3.	demon-controlled people are often weak and helpless when tormented by the spirit; and

4.	a large percentage of those tormented or occupied by this devil are unaware of this possession or refuse to acknowledge this existence.

Jesus's example: Jesus casts out demons out of several people in his healing ministry (Matt. 12:22–24).

Then was bought unto him and possessed with a devil blind and dumb and he healed him into much that the blind and dumb both spake and saw. (Matt. 12:22)

Another example is seen in Luke 8:27–39

Then went the devils out of the man, and the herd ran violently down a steep place into the lake and were choked. (Luke 8:33)

In both verses, Jesus cast out the demons from the people tormented, and they recovered completely from the sickness.

2.	Gods are not ignorant of the devil's devices.

	Lest Satan should get an advantage of us; for we are not ignorant of his devices. (2 Cor. 2:11)

3.	Gods know or should know the devil is under God's (Christ) control. Example in Job 1:6–12, Satan could not afflict Job except by God's permit. God rules over the entire world, whether heaven or earth. God is supreme over all; what we know determines how far we go in life and how battles are won.

	That the most high ruleth in the Kingdom of men, and giveth it to whomsoever he will and setteth up over it the basest of man. (Dan. 4:17b)

4.	Gods should know that we have victory over the devil.

Ye are God, little children, and have overcome them, because greater is he that is in you than he that is in the world. (1 John 4:4)

As gods, we can only exercise power and authority of the demons by casting them out, and they give us compliance or obey him when we know that Jesus is greater than devils, that we are, in turn, authorized by Jesus through the Holy Spirit to cast them.

5.   Gods must know that Jesus defeated the devils through His death.

Forasmuch then as the children are partakers of flesh and blood. He also himself likewise took part of the same, that though death he might destroy him that had the power of death that is the devil. (Heb. 2:14)

Gods need to resolve in our heart and soul the fact that the death of Jesus was the destruction of the power of devil over the lives of believers. Jesus, through death, gave us victory and dominion. This is wonderful.

6.   Jesus gave us power to become sons of God and also to cast out devils.

When the even was come they brought unto him many that were possessed with devils and he cast out the spirits with his word, and healed all that were sick. (Matt. 8:16)

7.   Gods have received power over unclean spirits.

And when he had called unto him his disciples, he gave them power against unclean spirits, to cast them out and to heal all manner of sickness and all manner of diseases.

8.   As gods, we should know that we are constantly at war with the devil. And also know our weapons are not canal.

For the weapons of our warfare are not canal but mightily through God to the pulling down of strongholds. (2 Cor. 10:4)

WARFARE DEVICES OF SATAN

Gods are not ignorant of the devices of Satan.

It is only a foolish combatant, warrior, or fighter that will underestimate the capability or capacity of his enemy. Individuals, communities, countries, and people all over the world engage in battles. Countries carry out espionage activities to ascertain the might of their enemies or competitors so as to defeat them when they come under battle. Careful planning and strategies of victory are made and are completed when the enemy dances and crafts are known. So also in the kingdom, God told us not be ignorant.

1. The serpent defeated Adam and Eve in the beginning through his subtlety.

    The serpent was more subtle than any beast of the field which the lord God has made. And he said unto the woman, yea hath God said, ye shall not eat of every tree of the garden. (Gen. 3:1)

    God does not want us to argue with the devil or unbelievers about our convictions in the Word of God. The Word of God should be only "Yes, Lord." Yes, Lord, and no controversies, no doubting at all. No debate at any time. Anything outside obedience and compliance is treated as disobedience and treason against God and punishable by death, except when we repent. Anything outside obedience is a sin.

    What is a sin? Sin is rebellion against God. It is going to the right or left away from the commandments of God.

2. The devil is a liar and deceiver.

He was a murderer from the beginning and abode not in the truth, because there is no truth in him. When he speaketh a lie, he speaketh of his own for he is a liar, and the father of it. (John 8:44b)

3.   He leads men to contradict and doubt the truth.

And supper (having) now ended, the devil having now put into the heart of Judas Iscariot Simons son, to betray him. (John 13:2)

4.   Gods should not allow Satan to tempt them to sin. Satan tempts man to sin.

And when the tempter (devil) come to him, he said if thou be the son of God, command that the stones be made bread. (Matt. 4:4)

Satan uses the same devices, strategies, and tactics he used against Adam, and succeeded. He brought the same model against Jesus. Satan believed like the world. "You don't change a winning strategy," a winning team, or a winning model. But Jesus defeated him and his crafty devices through the Word of God. Knowledge of the Word of God is very vital. Prayer cannot replace it; singing and praises can replace the knowledge of God. The Bible says,

Ye shall know the truth and the truth shall make you free.

Gods are not be confused. Satan uses confusion against the saints.

For God is got the author of confusion, but of peace, as in all churches of the saints. (1 Cor. 14:33)

As gods, the scripture warns us against confusion. The devil comes into the church with misunderstandings, confusion, and disaffections. Therefore, we ought to cast out such spirit through the door, because it brings sin and division in the faith.

Gods must partner with Jesus and not the devil.

Why partner with Jesus?

1.   Jesus is our defender or attorney.

      And if any man sin, we have an advocate with the father, Jesus Christ the righteous. (1 John 2:1)

2.   He, Jesus, has entered into heaven for us.

      For Christ is not entered into the holy places made with hands, which are the figures of the true: but into heaven itself now to appear in the presence of God for us. (Heb. 9:24)

Wow, what a fantastic scripture. This gives us a sense of relaxation, knowing that our master Jesus has entered in for us. This gives believers complete assurance of salvation, not only salvation, but also reconciliation, adoption, sonship, and confidence in Christ Jesus. We are safe at last.

Gods don't partner with the devil.

Why should we never partner with Satan?

The devil is a destroyer.

1.   He causes devastation and destruction of lives and properties.

      Be sober, be vigilant, because your adversary the devil, as a roaring lion, walketh about seeking whom he may devour. (1 Pet. 5:8)

2.   The devil afflicts people with disease.

So went Satan forth from the presence of the lord, and smote job with sores, boils from the sole of his foot unto his crown. (Job 2:7)

Another occasion is when Jesus was teaching in one of the synagogues:

And behold there was a woman which had a spirit of infirmities eighteen years, and was bowed together and could in no wise lift up himself. (Luke 13:11)

3.   Satan seeks to subtract the saint from the teachings of Jesus.

And the lord said, Simon, Simon behold Satan hath desired to have you, that he may gift you as wheat. (Luke 22:31)

Satan's plans are always to divert our attention from the Word of God to attend to suffering, pain, and sorrow. He uses carnal weapons such as addiction, loss of job, barrenness, etc. to cause disaffections in homes; but gods know his antics and tactics. We, like Job, should not be moved. Job said,

Through he slay me yet will I trust in him, but I will maintain mine own ways before him. (Job 13:15)

See it, say it, and set it (Mark 11:23).

Hosea 14, Joel 3:10

Weakness and down it is a battle of the mind.

Life and death are in the power of the tongue.

Let the weak say I am strong

Daniel had something to tell everybody—**brothers, kings, and people—Goliath stalling**.

Truth is stronger than **fault**. The truth speaks what the Spirit can see.

GODS LIVE FOREVER WITH AN EVERLASTING LIFE

FOREVER: Eternally, perpetually, everlastingly, endlessly, and always.

LIVE: Energetic, vital, vivid, existing, and conscious.

1. Gods are those who have accepted the original nature of God Almighty, filled with the Holy Spirit, and born again.

    Gods have the same attributes and nature of God.

    For God so loved the world that he gave his only begotten son, that whosoever believeth in him should not perish, but have everlasting life. (John 3:16)

2. Gods are not condemned.

    He that believeth on him is not condemned. (John 3:17b)

3. Gods follow the everlasting way.

    And see if there be any wicked way in me and lead me in the way everlasting. (Ps. 139:24)

4. Gods (born-again men) rely on Jehovah as our everlasting strength.

    Trust ye in the lord forever for in the lord Jehovah is everlasting strength. (Isa. 26:4)

5. Jehovah is our everlasting light.

    The sun shall be no more thy light by day; neither for brightness shall the moon and light unto thee, but the lord shall be unto thee an everlasting light, and thy God thy glory. (Isa. 60:19)

    Also in the book of Revelation, God revealed the final light:

And the city had no need of the sun, neither of the moon to shine in it for the glory of God did lighten it, and the lamb is the light thereof. (Rev. 21:23)

6.   Gods forsake this world and the things of the world.

And everyone that hath forsaken houses or brethren or sister, or father, or mother, or wife or children and lands for my names sake shall inherit everlasting life. (Luke 19:29)

7.   Gods are raised up at the last day.

And there is the (father) will of him that sent me, that everyone which seeth the son, and believeth on may have everlasting life; and I will raise him up at the last day. (John 6:40)

8.   Gods have everlasting consolation with Jesus Christ, our Savior and Redeemer.

Now our lord Jesus Christ himself, and God even our father; which hath loved us, and hath given us everlasting consolation and good hope through grace. (2 Thess. 2:16)

TRANSFORMATION FROM MAN TO GOD THROUGH THE HOLY SPIRIT

HOLINESS: This is the only attribute of Jehovah God that singles Him out of all other names named.

True holiness is in conformity with real nature of Almighty God. The will of God becomes the prerequisite for accessary everybody's level of holiness. How much of the will of God is practiced in one's life and also how yielded we are in times of trials and tribulations goes a long way to prove the quality of brokenness in one's life.

Holiness is how distinguished a saint is from the unrenewed, **unreported world** and is not conformed to their principles and precepts, nor **governed** by their customs and maxims.

Holiness is the very nature and strength of God—the ability to do what is good and just, what is right and fair, from and without variableness.

WHO IS THE HOLY SPIRIT?

The Holy Spirit is the third person in the Godhead—God the Father, the Son, and the Holy Spirit.

For there are three that bear record in heaven, the father, the word (Jesus) and the holy ghost; and these are one. (1 John 5:7)

The Father, the Son, and the Holy Ghost are one and agree.

HOW DOES THIS TRANSFORMATION HAPPEN?

1. By coming upon us.

   And the spirit of the lord will come upon thee and thou shall prophesy with them and shall be turned into another man. 1Sam 10:6

   When the Spirit of the holy comes upon the person, He changes the entire disposition and outlook of that person. He or she becomes a new creation. He transforms us into another man, a man of God.

   Another scripture states,

   The spirit of the lord god is upon me, because the lord had anointed me to preach good tidings unto the meek. (Isa. 61:1A)

2. He creates a new heart and the right spirit along with a clean heart.

Create in me a clean heart O God, and renew a right spirit within me. (Ps. 51:10)

The Holy Spirit renews our commitment and relationship with God, which was severed because of disobediences. He is the new spirit that we receive at salvation. When the Holy Ghost comes into our life, the evil spirit exits our life.

ENTER THE HOLY GHOST, EXIT THE DEVIL

3.   Holy Ghost transforms us by giving us a closer relationship with Jesus.

Even the spirit of truth whom the world cannot because it seeteth him not, neither knoweth him. But ye know him. For he dwelleth with upon and shall be in you. (John 14:17)

Jesus explains the peculiarity of the Holy Spirit:

i.   The Spirit of truth and not lies.

ii. The sinners of the world cannot receive him, not knoweth him.

iii. He shall dwell with those who believe and receive Jesus and the message of salvation.

4.   We are transformed when we are filled by the Holy Spirit.

And be nor drunk with wine, wherein is excess, but be filled with the Holy Spirit. (Eph. 5:18)

We are to be filled with the Holy Spirit and not with wine or pride. God does not expect us to live life of excessive carousing, drugs, drinking, parting, etc. When we are filled with the Holy Ghost, we shall be inhabited by Him

5.   Awake from the dead.

Wherefore he saith, awake thou that sleepest and arise from the dead, and Christ shall give the light. (Eph. 5:14)

6.   He gives us life of peace.

For those that are after the flesh do mind the things of the flesh; But they that are after the spirit the things of the spirit. (Rom. 8:5)

Again,

To be carnally minded is death; but to be spiritually minded is life and peace. (Rom. 8:6)

So then, that are carnally minded and cannot please God. They can only please themselves and the devil.

7.   The spirit transforms us to virtuous men and women in Christ.

But the fruits of the spirit love, joy, peace longsuffering, gentleness, goodness, faith, meekness, temperance against such there is no law. (Gal. 5:22–23)

The Holy Ghost separates us from the thief, which comes not but to do evil.

The thief cometh not, but for to steal, to kill, and to destroy. (John 10:10A)

We are redeemed from this kind of spirit. The spirit of the Antichrist, the spirit of the devil, and are filled with the Spirit of God that giveth life.

I am come that they might have life, and that they might have it more abundantly. (John 10:10b)

We have the fruits of the spirit, namely LOVE, JOY, PEACE, LONG-SUFFERING, GOODNESS, GENTLENESS, FAITH, MEEKNESS, AND TEMPERANCE. All these combinations in the life of a man have transformed him to God, because it is all the fruit listed above, including others brought in through the Holy Spirit's interaction with us. This fruits of holiness help us take care of issues in our marriage, office, home, and other everyday chores of life.

8.   We become hopeful and not hopeless. Hopelessness has led to suicide, divorce, separation, and even death. But we are full of hope in Christ Jesus.

> **And again Esarias saith, there shall be a root of Jesse, and he that shall rise to reign over the gentiles, in him shall the gentiles trust.** (Rom. 15:12)

9.   The Holy Spirit transforms when He gives us different kinds of spiritual gifts.

> **For to one is given by the spirit the word of wisdom, to another the word of knowledge by the same spirit; to another, faith by the same spirit; to another the working miracles; to another prophecy; to another discerning of spirits; to another drivers kinds of tongues; to another interpretation of tongues.** (1 Cor. 12:8–10)

The diverse gifts are useful for us as individuals and families of Christ. It is for the edification of the church. People need miracles, signs and wonders, to cope with everyday life activities. The gifts also differentiate us from ordinary men. The Bible called them more man. This are men who wear image of God like a clothing (physical body) but don't have the likeness (Spirit) of God. They cannot have this gift because they cannot become the Holy Ghost. Holy Ghost is for everybody who receives Christ as Lord and Savior, but not everybody can receive Christ, so the Holy Ghost cannot be given to them.

GODS MUST POSSESS THE FRUITS OF THE SPIRIT

But the fruits of the spirit love, Joy, peace, longsuffering, gentleness, goodness, faith, meekness, temperance, against such there is no law.

1. LOVE: Unselfish concern for other persons. Look at 1 Corinthians 13:4–7.

   Agape love—unconditional.

   This means to love God supremely and love others unselfishly; these are the two very important commands Jesus gave His disciples. It means to love unconditionally. This is the kind of love that wins exemplified by Jesus when he died on the cross. We also should emulate this.

   Love is scarce today in the world. When we show love to people that hate us and don't show hatred back, they become connected to our faith.

2. JOY: Great delight or positive feeling being excited about something or somebody. A believer's spiritual joy is produced by the Holy Spirit. This joy is deeper than just been happy. It remains happy all the time.

   In that hour Jesus rejoiced in the spirit and said. (Luke 10:21A)

   The joy from the spirit does not look at circumstances. It is not bipolar. No mood swings or depression. It is permanent and trusted because it is a gift of the Holy Ghost.

3. PEACE: Harmony, accord, tranquility, conciliation, contentment. This state is brought about by cordial relationships or reconciliations. Peace has its root from God. There is worldly peace, but the peace discussed here is the one that comes from the Holy Ghost.

   And the peace of God that passeth understanding shall keep

your hearts and minds through Christ Jesus. (Phil. 4:7)

4.   Longsuffering

5.   Gentleness

6.   Goodness

7.   Faith

8.   Meekness

9.   Temperance

Galatians 5:22 **Birthday**

When you practice the fruit of the Spirit, nothing can work against you (1 Cor. 13:1).

The nature of God sets us from the enemy.

What works for us; what is **against** the devil?

The fruit of the Spirit is the lifestyle of God's love. It is giving us His **undying** self so that we also become **covenant** and **approach** to **prove any circumstance**. The fruit of Spirit gives us **control in life,** a **way** into him, **churches,** and repay back God's **nation**. The fruit of the Spirit is the power of God that enable us to be gods. Love is the **exchange of affection, tangible fame, and goodness of God. Penance of God hath behave attached.**

Joy—Intensity of gladness bigger than us, **overwhelming us**.

Joy is who God is, and your response to God is elation, wonder, **close file** in something or somebody. **I am regocery baking God is on my side**.

Peace—Calm, restful, freedom from disturbance, inclination to **have** calm, free from strife, composed.

Patience—Able to persevere under pressure with a good mind and heart. Having a calm expectation being in a quiet.

Kindness—Being thoughtful, loving another, showing **simple quality of grace**.

Goodness—Favorable toward someone, giving people a **down endurance**.

Faithful—Consistent, constant in **your promise, trusting and keeping the word**.

Gentleness—Meekness, strength, **and self-control, tenderhearted, overcoming**.

Self-control—Restraint, exercising control. Having moderate control of people.

These are attributes God practices in relations to us.

The Questions

1.   How does this fruit work against the enemy?

2.   Is practicing the fruit better than the gift?

3.   Everything the enemy tries to bring against us works for us.

When you work in a negative way, you work in opposition to yourself.

God wants us to be more than conquerors by working in the fruits of the Spirit.

By practicing the fruit of the Spirit, you can demoralize the enemy with your goodness, gentleness, love, and joy.

Against the fruit of the Spirit, nothing works against it.

Gods are temperate.

- Eternal

- Content

- Overwhelmed in your heart

- Possessed by joy

- Possessed by kindness

- Experience God in their emotion

- Feel God in their emotion

TEN THINGS GODS PRACTICE

1. Gods know God as their Father. God wants to make us happy, loving, and peaceful.

2. Gods practice the fruit of the Spirit.

3. Gods relate with God Almighty through the fruits of the Spirit.

4. Gods know people come to us to encounter the fruit of the Spirit.

5. Gods play games with God through the fruit of the Spirit.

6. Gods learn love through loving their enemies (Matt. 5:44).

The purpose of some **persecution** is to teach you how to bless.

Gods must possess and effectively use the gifts of the HOLY SPIRIT.

GIFT: A gift can be considered an endowment, legally, donation, bequest, subsidy, etc.

A gift is seen to be something donated, endowment from somebody to another. Sometimes it is merited or not, but is given anyways.

1. The gift of words of wisdom: Mark 13:11, Luke 12:11–12, John 14:26B

2. Word of knowledge

3. Faith: 1 Corinthians 12:9–10
    To another faith by the same spirit. (1 Cor. 12:9)

4. Working of miracles: 1 Corinthians 12:10

5. To another, the working miracles (1 Cor. 12:10).

6. Prophecy: 1 Corinthians 12:7a, 10; John 16:13b; Act 2:17–18

7. Discerning of spirit: Isaiah 11:23, 1 Corinthians 2:12–25, 1 Corinthians 12:10

8. Diverse kinds of tongues: Acts 2:1–4, 1 Corinthians 13:1

9. Interpretation of tongues: 1 Corinthians 14:4

The gift of the Holy Spirit are these bestowed freely by the Holy Spirit upon believers because we are His children.

Of his own will begat he us with the world of truth, that we should be a kind of first fruits of his creatures. (James 1:18)

Chapter 7

THE SECRET OF GOD; THE REWARD OF GODS, OR MAN

1. Be strong and courageous.

Be strong and of good courage. For unto this people shall thou divide for an inheritance the land which I sware unto their fathers to give them. (Josh. 1:6)

SECRET—Can be defined as something mysterious, arcane, cryptic, occult, mystical, veiled, obscure, hidden, shrouded, concealed, clandestine, stealthy, etc.

Secret:

1. Kept from public knowledge or from the knowledge of a certain person.

2. Witch awn, remote, secluded from general knowledge.

   Individuals have secrets; nations, companies, families, and even Christ had His secrets. God also has secrets.

3. SECRET OF WISDOM

   And that he will show (you) thee the secrets of wisdom. (Job 11:6)

4. The secret of deep things

   He revealeth the deep and secret things. (Dan. 2:22A)

5. He revealeth what is in darkness

   He knoweth what is in darkness. (Dan. 2:22A)

6. He revealeth the secret of witchcraft.

   He sitteth in the lurking places of the village.

7. He reavealeth the ways of murderers.

   In the secret places doth he murder the innocent? (Ps. 10:8)

Brothers and sisters, not anything we see that look right are right; the world is full of secrets.

1. Secret of the darkness

2. Secret of light

3. Secret of scene

4. Secrets of mystics

THE SECRET OF OBEDIENCE

Obedience: Dutiful, loyal, devoted faithful, submissive.

Obedience can be described as giving in to the orders or instructions of one in authority or control. Willingness to submit to authority or obey.

1.   Obedience to God in our duty

Fear God and keep his commandments; for this is the whole duty of man. (Eccles. 12:13b)

This is our duty and obligation to God for success.

2.   Obey wholeheartedly

Give me understanding and, I shall keep thy law, yea I shall observe it with my whole heart. (Ps. 119:34)

3.   Obey in all things without reservations

Ye shall observe to do therefore as the lord your God hath commanded you. Ye shall bot turn aside to the right hand or to the left. (Deut. 5:32)

Obedience is straightforward, not according to our own feeling. Today, some people obey God in the way they feel. Sometimes they interpret scriptures to favor their sinful ways. They say God will understand.

2.   God knows better.

3.   I have tried and pushed, but God allows it for a purpose. Some even say, "All things work together for good," and the Bible stories support their mischief. Do be like that. Jesus Christ declared,

Let your ye be ye and your nay be nay for any other they is off the devil.

BENEFITS OF OBEDIENCE OR SECRETS OF SUCCESS THROUGH OBEDIENCE

1. BLESSINGS, NOT CURSES.

    Behold, I set before you this day a blessing and a curse. A blessing if ye obey the commandments of the lord your God, which I command you today. (Deut. 11:26–27)

2. Blessings of prosperity/good success.

    But. Thou shall meditate therein day and night, that thou mayest observe to do according to all that is written therein; for then thou shall make thy way prosperous and then thou shall have good success. (Josh. 1:8b)

3. Blessing of good success is also included.

    And then thou shall have good success.

4. Blessing of soul's redemption. Many people become saved through our own obedience.

    For as by one man's disobedience, many where sinners, so by the obedience of one man, many be made righteous. (Rom. 5:19)

5. Spiritual blessings of obedience and submission.

    i. We become peculiar treasure unto God.

    Now therefore, if ye will obey my voice indeed and keep my (commandment) covenant, them ye shall be a peculiar (people) treasure unto me above all people; for all the earth

is mine. (Exod. 19:5)

ii.   Obedience brings happiness.

If ye know these things happy are ye if ye do them. (John 13:17)

iii.   Obedience makes us friends of God.

Ye are my friends if ye do whatsoever I command you. (John 15:14)

Soul purification is found in obedience.

Seeing ye have purified your sows in obeying the truth. (1 Pet. 1:22)

4.   MATERIAL BLESSING IN OBEDIENCE

1.   The best is in obedience

If ye be will and obedient, ye shall eat the good of the land. (Isa. 1:19)

2.   Obedience brings prosperity and pleasure

If they obey and serve him, thy shall spend their days in prosperity, and their years in pleasure. (Job 36:11)

3.   Obedience brings deliverance

But Jeremiah said, thy shall not deliver thee, obey, I beseech thee the voice of the lord, which I speak unto thee, so it shall be well unto thee, and thy soul shall live. (Jer. 38:20)

Protection through obedience makes gods immortal and invincible.

1.   1. God become every to our enemies

But if thou shall indeed obey his voice and do all that I speak. I shall become enemies unto thine enemies.

2.   Advisory to our adversaries

Evil an advisory unto thine adversaries. (Exod. 23:22)

3.   Obedience guarantee our safety

Wherefore ye shall do my (will) statutes and keep my judgements and do them; and ye shall dwell in the level in safety. (Lev. 25:18)

Chapter 8

God's Attributes/Man's Blueprint

THE BLUEPRINT 1: GOD'S HOLINESS

Holy, holy, holy is the Lord God, Almighty, who was and is and is to come. (Rev. 4:8)

Holiness: True holiness consist in a conformity to the nature and will of God, whereby a saint is distinguished from the unrenewable world and is not actuated by their principles and precepts nor governed by their maxims and customs.

There are different degree of holiness in the saints, but sincerity is inseparable from the being of it.

The fourth chapter and verse 8 of the book of Revelations opens our eyes to the stable nature of God before existence, now and forever. God is holy and will forever be holy.

What is Holiness?

Holiness is a state of being holy. Without blemish or sin, deep state righteousness and transparency. Without worldly vices that lead to death. Anything that does not bring conviction in the law court and is devoid of human blame or rejection is holy.

WHO IS LIKE UNTO THEE, O LORD, AMONG THE GODS WHO IS LIKE THEE, GLORIOUS IN HOLINESS, FEARFUL IN PRAISES, DOING WONDERS? (Exod. 15:11)

These was a song just immediately after God's miraculous deliverance from Egypt. The Israelites saw the mighty power of JEHOVAH GOD and how He dealt with Pharaoh and his army. They playback the process and negotiations between God and Pharaoh, the opportunities given to the Egyptians to let the Israelites go in peace without a fight.

Glorious in holiness: Depicts God's long suffering and ability to exercise family patience, reorganizing the fact that intermarriages had occurred and mixed multitudes are imagined. But there is a difference between fair play and firm play, which God does apply when dealing with humans. The plagues and the **fiman showdown** came to show God's firmness in letting the people go to confirm His promise to Abraham.

As the image and the likeness of God, born again, Holy Ghost-filled believers are expected to manifest their important attributes of God. Holiness, integrity, transparency, and fairness separate God and His Son from other deity. The Spirit of God is called the Holy Spirit. God is holiness personified.

The holy attributes of God make us know God hates sin but admonishes sinners to repent. God expects us not to sin or even entertain those who are involved. This attributes of holiness were so important and is still very important today. Jesus told His disciples to want for the baptism of the Holy Spirit.

AND BEING assembled together with them, commanded them that they should not from Jerusalem, but wait for the promise of the father. (Acts 1:4)

Jesus was reminding us of what was written in another scripture in the Old Testament by Prophet Joel:

AND IT SHALL COME TO PASS afterward that I will pour out my spirit upon all flesh, and your sons and your daughters shall prophesy your old men shall dream dreams and your young shall see visions. (Joel 2: 28)

When the Holy Spirit came upon disciples, they became energized; they received the following godly power or nature hitherto absent:

1. Sealed:

    Who hath also sealed us, and given us the earnest of the spirit in our hearts (2 Cor. 1:22).

2. He quickened us expect us to quicken unbelievers (John 6:63).

    It is the spirit that quickened

    Agreed the Spirit quickened, but through our prayers, laying on of hands, and evening exhortation, people receive the Holy Ghost. Example: Acts 19:2–5.

    And when Paul had laid his hands upon them, Holy Ghost came upon them and them spake with tongues and prophesied. (Acts 19:6)

Another scenario is in Acts 8:15–17; Samaritans received baptism of the Holy Spirit after salvation. We are common to preach the gospel so people can receive the Holy Ghost and live right.

Now when the Apostle which were at Jerusalem heard that Samaria had received the Word of God, they sent unto them Peter and John;

Then laid they hands on them and received the Holy Ghost.

The Holy Spirit is a person, and His nature is holiness. He brings all the other attributes with Him. Whom He comes and lived well, any man, that man becomes a supernatural being.

Example, Peter: Peter was a timid man, a betrayer, a weakling, quick to act, slow to think, jealous of John, lack understanding, and overambitious but with no knowledge. But after the baptism of the Holy Spirit in Act 2:2–4:

And suddenly there came a sound from heaven as of a rushing mighty wind and it filed all the house where they were sitting.

And there appeared unto them chore tongues like as of fire and it sat upon each of them. And they were all filled with the Holy Ghost and began to speak with other tongues as the spirit gave them utterances.

So God's Spirit is given to us whom we are served. So when we sin with others, they relieve a deposit of God.

God's holiness defines sin. Through God's holiness, the world now has a standard to measure with. Sin is sin, whether it is the transgression of a prostitute or the iniquity of an idol worshiper in African or human sacrifice in Israel or the terrorist attach of the jihadist. Sin is black and considered to be error in the sight of God.

God is the sum total of perfection, excellence, purity, and transparency. God's holiness is who He is. Man is expected, through Jesus Christ washing with the blood and Holy Spirit, to become holy like God through imitation. God's love is moral and holy; it ensures evil cannot touch us.

God lives in holiness. His throne is in holiness. His judgment is in holiness. God's discipline or justice is in holiness. God's attribute because of holiness function in perfection balance. When we weigh other variables, we find God to be who He says He is. Just GOD.

BLUEPRINT 2: GOD'S GRACE

The grace of God is the gift of God to man, To man who are lost and don't know the way back. Grace is defined most times by preachers as unmerited favor, something given despite receiving lack of gratitude, insolence, and lack of sensitivity to good work.

The scriptures says,

For it is by grace you have been saved, through faith and this not from yourselves, It is the gift of God. (Eph. 2:8)

The next verse actually explains the condition of the grace. This is very controversial today. It has bought a lot of teachings to grace.

Example, (1) some preach that grace does not need any man's input at all to be effective (Eph. 2:8), and (2) schools claim it is a collaboration of thought and partnership with God that makes grace work effectively, and they **good.**

Grace is seen as the free and unmerited, eternal nature of God. This is by His favor and goodwill. This is the spring and service of all the benefit man receives from God.

And if by grace, then is it no more of works. Other grace is no more grace. But if it be of works, otherwise grace is no more grace. But if it be of works, then is it no more grace; otherwise work is no more book. (Rom. 11:6)

The above scripture implies a total free gift package for man. Man was not involved in the planning, neither will man be so involved in its execution. The call of God is a holy calling through grace.

Who had saved us and called us with a holy calling not according to our works but according to his own purpose and grace which was given us in Christ Jesus before the world began. (2 Tim. 1:9)

Since the grace of God is free. Believers should share this grace with all mankind. Before sharing, man must first a course this grace. You cannot give what you don't have, they say. Grace implies giving without strings attached. Doing without expecting payback. Loving selflessly and unconditionally. God's benevolence opulence—charitable, inclination to do good.

The grace of God shows God's opulence—much wealth, property, abundant nature. God's profusion and luxuriant attribute is passed on to us, His children.

We as the image and likeness of God also should demonstrate God's kind of nature of excessive well of abundance without fear of scarcity or lack and, by so doing, attracting others to the kingdom of God.

Freely, freely you have secured; freely, freely give.

BLUEPRINT 3: GOD'S MERCY—COMPASSION

The lord is compassionate and gracious, slow to anger, abounding in love … As a father has compassion on his children. So the lord has compassion on those who fear him. For he knows how we are formed. He remember that we are dust. (Ps. 103:8, 13–14)

God's mercy expresses compassion of God. The mercy of God talks of God's salvation. What is mercy? Refraining from harming or punishing offender enemies, person, in one's power. It also means kindness in excess of what may be expected or demanded by us.

Mercy, according to the definition, implies to refrain from punishing or harming an offender.

When man fell in Genesis 3, the whole mankind became offenders in the sight of God. Everybody became doomed to die. Generations plunge into eternal damnation, and God needed to hatch a plan to save man, so He said Genesis 3:15,

And I will put enmity between thee and the woman and between thy seed and her seed, it shall bruise his heel.

With this statement, God declared war on the kingdom of darkness and developed a salvation and redemption plan for mankind.

The battle line was drawn; the die was cast, and the process had begun. God brought in other salvation strategies. These were just a foreshadow of His original plan. These include the following:

1.   Salvation from Egypt in hand of pharaoh.

2.   The ark of the covenant of Noah.

3.   The ten commandment.

4.   The temple worship, the tabernacle, holiest of holiest, the mercy seat, and the blood of bulls for atonement

All these are a foreshadow of what is to come: Jesus. God's plan was for an appointed time, and at the time appointed, Jesus emerged to finish that which was started and redeem man completely.

SALVATION means saving or being saved from danger, difficulty, or destruction. Rescue from death or calamity.

For all have sinned and come short of the glory of God. (Rom. 3:23)

Everybody living on earth; after Adam and Eve fell, all become sinners. Every attempt to do good was met with frustration, depression, and utter futility. The writer of Ecclesiastes 7:20 yelled,

Not a just man on earth that doeth good and sinneth not.

Romans 3:10 bluntly declares, "**There is not righteous no not one.**"

SALVATION BY THE WORK OF THE LAW

God gave Moses the law as a temporary remedy for man's excesses. The law was holy, but it was unable to save anybody. The frustration was these and pam. People still need a permanent relief from their situation—a temporary relief like taking aspirin, antidepressant, or opium to numb man. That can give nothing compared to what God had planned for man. The inadequately of the law was expressed in James 2:10:

For whatsoever shall keep the whole law, and yet offered in one point, he is guilty of all.

SALVATION AND MERCY ONLY THROUGH JESUS

The scripture declared that,

Neither is there salvation in any other, for there is none other name under heaven given among men whereby we must be served. (Acts 4: 12)

Furthermore, Jesus declared,

For God so loved the world He gave his only begotten son that whosoever believeth in him should not perish but have everlasting life. (John 3:16)

We are the image and the likeness of God. Jesus's declaration is to keep us be reconciled to God and then be free from the curse of death. This saving nature goes with compassion for souls. Knowing that souls that don't come to Christ will perish.

He that believeth not shall not see life. (John 3:36b)

Also If ye believe not that I am he ye shall die in your sins. (John 8:24)

The SMS or SOS is urgent. We need to sound the alarm and blow the trumpet of rescue.

THE GENESIS OF THE ISSUE

In the creations of God, there were so many beautiful and pleasant creatures, mammal, and nature. But there was terminal in complete until Genesis 1:26:

AND God said let us make man in our image, after our likeness and let them have dominion over the fish of the sea, and over the fowl of the air, and over the cattle, and over all the earth ,and over every creeping thing that creepeth upon the earth.

According to our text, God the Father, the Son, and the Holy Spirit agreed on the terms of the making of man; what he will look like; its composure, gender, area of operation; and his authority and dominion. It is very obvious that God had a very robust plan of creation and a very good plan for man that He decided to create him last after other creatures had been created. Sweet, I say, so God proceeded to create man, and the next verse confirmed that:

And God created man in his own image, in the image of God created he him, male and female created he them. (Gen. 1:27)

1.   Please notice that in verse 26, God used the word *make—*

meaning, there is a process in the making of man to become something else other than that created. But in verse 27, the Bible used the word *create*, which means that an aspect of the making had being completed.

2. Secondly, two words (verb) were used in verse 26—*image* and *likeness* were used to explain God's plan. But in the actual creation only image was accomplished. The likeness was the next process.

    Subsequent verses now told how God blessed them and commanded them to be fruitful, multiply, and replenish the earth. But they were just the image of God and yet to be Him in likeness.

    Why, the process for the likeness of God and finish the job became was for another time. It takes a different process. This process was supposed to be a conscious one.

WHY?

1. They were created asleep, but they will be made a life.

2. They were created adults, but they will be by being children.

3. They were given freedom to dominate the earth, but they will earn it through loyalty and obedience.

4. They were commented on what to do and not to do, but the choice relied on them.

5. They were created to look like God physically. Emotional and spiritual likeness must be a choice.

Chapter 9

THE FALL OF MAN

The story of the fall of man in Genesis 3:1–7 was said that anytime I read it, I feel deep anger for the First Adam's very cheap fall and for the childish antics of the devil.

Well, couldn't the Bible itself say that the serpent was more subtle than any beast of the (sea) field, which God had created (Gen. 3:1A).

Nevertheless, the fall of man was so painful that it appears Adam didn't know the following:

1. Who he was in God.

2. He didn't understand the enmity between God and the serpent because of his lies.

3. He didn't understand the enmity and jealousy of devil over his creation. Adam refused to intimate his wife about the consequences of letting a stranger into their domain or realm.

4. Adam failed to pray and prophesy even during and after the incident.

5. Adam and Eve refused to repent and seek for forgiveness from God. Rather, they started trading blames.

6.   Adam did not know that Satan was a murderer and a liar (John 8:44).

ADAM'S IGNORANCE OF WHO HE WAS IN GOD

In Genesis 1:26, God's intention was clear in His creative plan. God said,

LET US MAKE MAN IN OUR IMAGE, AFTER OUR LIKENESS. AND LET THEM HAVE DOMINION OVER FISH OF THE SEA, AND OVER THE FOULS OF THE AIR AND OVER THE CATTLES, AND OVER ALL THE EARTH, AND OVER EVERY CREEPING THING THAT CREEPETH UPON THE EARTH. (GEN. 1:26)

And the next verse of scripture confirmed that

AND GOD CREATED MAN IN HIS OWN IMAGE AND LIKENESS AND IN THE IMAGE OF GOD CREATED HE HIM, MALE AND FEMALE CREATED HE THEM. (Gen. 1:27)

Man was created to exercise power and authority over everything God had created, including the serpent himself. But man was ignorant and therefore fell woefully to a very cheap disguise of the enemy.

ENMITY BETWEEN GOD AND SATAN

This enmity between God and Satan, the devil, had existed before creation. This jealousy led to a war in heaven, and Satan lost the battle (see Ezekiel 37).

SATAN'S JEALOUSY OVER ADAM'S CREATION

It was obvious that Satan was jealous over the creation of Adam and the dominion given to him to control and be supreme over everything, including him, the devil.

This lack of proper, adequate evaluation of this mammon led to a very serious slack on the part of Adam and Eve, called complacency.

THE SERPENT WAS THE MOST SUBTLE THAN ANY BEAST OF THE FIELD THAT GOD HAD CREATED.

Gen. 3:1A. The serpent here was unmasked by Jesus and described or regarded as a personality in Matthew 4:1–10.

THEN JESUS WAS LED UP TO THE SPIRIT INTO THE WILDERNESS TO BE TEMPTED OF THE DEVIL. (Matt. 4:1)

Notice in verse 3, Jesus referred to Satan as he.

AND WHEN THE TEMPTER CAME TO HIM, HE SAID, "If Thou be the Son of God."

Satan is a liar. He used the same tactics and scheme that worked against Adam and Eve against Jesus. The scheme is still in use today. This scheme is so perfected and trusted that it still works today—disguise of evil intent and ability to play, false concern, empathy, friendliness, and persistence. Satan used mature psyche and evil profiling to be.

Adam and Eve coupled with so much lies. Enough to arouse and give false motivation and encouragement to break the law of a sovereign God, if necessary.

This is a shame. Shame the satanic scheme, plot, devour, or design still works today and is robbing gods of their freedom and sovereign authority. Dominion is God through Christ Jesus.

The Bible calls the devices of the enemy:

FOR WE ARE NOT IGNORANT OF THE DEVICES OF THE ENEMY.

ADAM AND EVE FAILED TO PRAY. There was no record that Adam and Eve prayed before and after the incident. The Bible did say that when God appeared in the evening, they were hiding themselves (verse 8).

AND THE HEARD THE VOICE OF THE LORD GOD WALKING IN THE GARDEN IN THE COOL OF THE DAY; AND ADAM AND THE WIFE HID THEMSELVES FROM THE PRESENCE

OF THE LORD GOD FROM AMONGST THE TREES OF THE GARDEN. (GEN 3:8)

ADAM AND EVE FAILED (REFUSE) TO REPENT.

Despite all the opportunity given to them to come straight before God and repent of their sin, Adam decided to trade blame on the gift of God, his wife; and Eve also decided to blame the serpent, who didn't see anybody to blame, but rather rejoiced by taking away the dominion.

See Genesis 3:12: **"AND THE MAN SAID, THE WOMAN WHOM THOU GAVEST ME BE WITH ME OF THE TREE AND I DID EAT."**

God then confronted the woman, and here is His answer:

AND THE LORD GOD SAID UNTO THE WOMAN, WHAT IS THIS THAT THOU HAST DONE? AND THE WOMAN SAID, THE SERPENT BEQUILED ME AND I DID EAT. (GEN 3:13)

God became angry and furious because there was no opportunity to quickly amend the problem. He was not given the opportunity to save the situation. Having seen the DEFEAT OF ADAM, God quickly postponed steps to salvage the remaining part by introducing the redemption PLAN, hence the fall of man was completed.

CONSEQUENCES OF ADAM'S FALL

1.   **Death came to the world.**

Death is also decrease, demise, mortality, or expiration. Death is the end of physical existence of a man, animals, creatures, and everything that by exist with life on the inside.

Death is actually the price human pay for their soul, disobedience, and rebellion against God.

IN THE SWEAT OF THE FACE SHALT, THOU EAT BREAD, TILL THOU RETURN UNTO GROUND; FOR OUT OF IT WAS THOU TAKEN; FOR DUST THOU ART, AND UNTO DUST SHALL THOU RETURN. (GEN. 3:19)

INTRODUCE

This course brought death into the world, and subsequently, man lost his right to life. His fellowship with God was broken; man is corrupt with a deadly virus—seen inside man. He can no longer abide with man in the Garden of Eden, in paradise. Listen to what God said:

AND THE LORD GOD SAID, BEHOLD THE MAN IS BECOME AS ONE OF US (DEVIL) TO GOOD AND EVIL; AND NOW, LEST HE PUT FORTH HIS HAND AND TAKE ALSO OF THE TREE OF LIFE (JESUS), AND EAT AND LIVE FOREVER. (GEN. 3:22)

God's intent was for man to live forever, but not in a fallen state, corrupt and with sin. No, God cannot compromise His nature. No sinner shall live forever with God. God had to imitate the plan to bring solution to this precentor situation.

With this words, God rolled out his plan to bring HIS SON, JESUS, to redeem us from the curses and effects of sin. God said,

AND I WILL PUT ENMITY BETWEEN THEE AND THE WOMAN, AND BETWEEN THY SEED AND HER SEED; IT SHALL BRUISE THE HEAD AND THOU SHALL BRUISE HIS HEEL. (GEN. 3:15)

Our heavenly father quickly communicated His plan and agenda for man. His plan of salvation and eternal life was provided for those who believe in the son of the woman that Satan beguiled and disgraced. This is through the atoning death of Jesus Christ. Romans 6:23 says,

FOR THE WAGES OF SINS IS DEATH, BUT THE GIFT OF GOD IS ETERNAL LIFE THROUGH JESUS CHRIST OUR LORD.

2.   **Man became debased.**

DEBASED, REPROBATE, DEPRIVED

Man became a person who is deprived. He or she lost the attributes of God. Man lost the nature of his original creation and became reprobate, corrupt, or worthless.

This is a term used for those who reject God or those who are rebellious to the authority of God. Look at Romans 1:28:

Even as they do not like to retain God in their knowledge. God gave them over to a reprobate (debased) mind to do those things which are not convenient.

And what are those debased, worthless things unexpected of gods or people of this caliber?

Let us see verse 29:

BEING FILLED WITH ALL UNRIGHTEOUSNESS, MALICIOUSNESS, FORNICATION, WICKEDNESS, COVETOUSNESS, FALL OF ENVY, MURDER DEBATE, DECEIT MALIGNITY, WHISPERERS.

This continued in verses 30–31:

BACKBITERS, HATERS OF GOD, DESPITEFUL, PROUD, BOASTERS. INVENTORS OF EVIL THINGS, DISOBEDIENT TO PARENTS; WITHOUT UNDERSTANDING, COVENANT BREAKERS, WITHOUT NATURAL AFFECTION, IMPLACABLE, UNMERCIFUL.

These are also some of the attributes of a debased life, a life totally bankrupt and devoid of light and life of God. The consequence of this kind of life is clearly written in verse 32:

WHO KNOWING THE JUDGEMENT OF GOD, THAT THEY WHICH COMMIT SUCH THINGS ARE WORTHY OF DEATH.

Now check this out. The Bible say not just people who do likewise or also corrupt themselves, but rather

NOT ONLY DO THE SAME, BUT HAVE PLEASURE IN THEM THAT DO THEM. (Rom. 1:3B)

As gods or idols of God, we are not expected to live a debased but victorious life.

SEPARATION FROM GOD IS PAINFUL

SEPARATION—DISUNION, SEGREGATION, DISCONNECTION, SEQUESTRATION.

When Adam and Eve fell into sin, they experience a disconnection from the original source, which was God Almighty's likeness. Everyone who rebel against the hegemony of God automatically experience a SEQUESTRATION from God, which led to pain, anguish, and suffering. Most times, it can be eternal. If not check, we look at the following scriptures:

1.   **INIQUITIES AND SIN**

BUT YOUR INIQUITIES HAVE SEPARATED BETWEEN YOU AND YOUR GOD, AND YOUR SINS HAVE HID HIS FACE FROM YOU, THAT HE WILL NO HEAR. (ISA. 59:2)

In this verse, we can identify iniquities and SIN as the reasons of unanswered prayer and God's inability to help man in certain situations, thereby causing separation.

2.   **Romans 8:38–39 reads,**

FOR I AM PERSUADED, THAT NEITHER DEATH, NOR LIFE, NOR ANGELS, NOR PRINCIPALITIES, NOR POWERS, NOR THINGS PRESENT, NOR THINGS TO COME, NOR HEIGHT, NOR DEPTH, NOR ANY OTHER CREATURE SHALL BE ABLE TO SEPARATE US FROM THE LOVE OF GOD WHICH IS IN CHRIST JESUS OUR LORD.

Several people are hindered from attaining their full potential due to things enumerated above in the two verses.

HINDRANCES MENTIONED INCLUDE the following:

1.   DEATH

2.   LIFE

3.   ANGELS

4.   PRINCIPALITIES

5.   POWERS

6.   HEIGHT

7.   DEPTH

8.   CREATURES KNOWN OR UNKNOWN—DEVILS

These things enumerated consist fear to a lot of people, including believers. The Bible say fear brings torment. This torment most times lead to depression. Gods are not supposed to fear at all because Jesus conquered fear. But separation from the Father, Jesus takes away the confidence we have and plunged man into darkness. Like Adam, their eyes became open to see the imminent danger. They saw they were exposed.

CRY TO PAIN

When Jesus was separated momentarily from the Father on the cross, He cried out:

AND ABOUT THE NINTH HOUR JESUS CRIED WITH A LOUD VOICE, SAYING ELI ELI LAMA SABACTHANI, THAT'S TO SAY MY GOD MY GOD WHY THOU HAST FORSAKEN ME. (Matt. 27:46)

At the moment, when Jesus paid the price of removing or taking away the SINS of the world, the Bible says,

HE BECAME SIN FOR US WHO KNEW NO SIN THAT THE BLESSING OF ABRAHAM.

At this point, God was separated from Him. Jesus cried out because He LOVED GOD SO MUCH and couldn't bear the emptiness and barrenness, pain and unworthiness of been separated from God for the first time. Jesus died completely.

JESUS, OUR HIGH PRIEST

Jesus became a high priest for us to make us children of God.

Christ also glorified not Himself to be made a high priest but Him that said unto Him, **"Thou art my son, today have I begotten thee"** (Heb. 5:5).

Jesus's priesthood was ordained and sanctioned by God, and God made Him a priest:

"Thou art a priest forever of the order of mechies-edes." (Heb. 5:6b)

As a priest in this order, Jesus was made higher than the angels. Yet for us, they hang on the cross or tree for us so that we can enjoy the blessings of God.

Whom in the days of his flesh when he had offered up prayers, and supplications with strong crying and tears unto him that was able to save him from death and was heard in that he feared. (Heb. 5:7)

GODS ATTRIBUTE / MANS BLUEPRINT

The attribute of God can be defined as a quality or characteristic of (somebody) a person (peculiar to one) or thing. To set down or think of as belonging to produce by, resulting from or originating in.

Another keyword in this subhead is *blueprint*, an exact or detailed plan or outline.

We shall look at different attributes of God Almighty, that peculiar quality or characteristics that God expects to see in man.

Man is made in God's image, after His likeness. Therefore, whatever are the attributes of God must reflect created them, and he found out they were good.

The attributes of God are important, and the knowledge of it can help remove the following:

1.   Have a better view of God, who He really is; you need to know He is self-sufficient and good.

2.   God sets kings, mayors, presidents, legislators, and even school teachers in authority. And that He needs your obedience.

3.   That all manner of vices or ills in the society attend a low view of God.

4.   That God is very potent and powerful, and you or your family rely solely on Him; He will make difficult situation lighter.

His yoke is Easy and his body is Light.

5.   Salvation is very free; at least receiving the partnership in maintaining this salvation still anchors on effective collaboration between you and God. Most times, 95 percent to 5 percent ignorance of this may make us struggle with difficult situations all alone.

6.   Our view of God affects the whole facet of our being. Ignorance of this very important thing affects church growth, business, personal endeavor, and other life endeavors.

7.   No church or family, institution or country can rise above the view its people hold of God.

8.   The vision of any man, nation, or institution can never be greater than the view personal hold of God.

9.   The knowledge of God's attributes, which is man's exact blueprint, nature, addresses a lot of misconceptions about who God really is. Today, spirituality may bring to mind yoga, trace dental medication, witchcraft, voodoo, etc.

In India today, we have over 1 billion idols called gods.

In China, eastern religion

In Africa

Middle East, Islam, Marabouts

Whimsical or grotesque view of God is seen or heard in different quarters today on TV, churches, monasteries, shrines, people, and races. Individuals are sometimes immortalized and worshipped as gods or idols.

1. Today, Christian equate the devil—Satan—as being on the same pedestal with God or sometimes even bigger. This is reflected in their outlook, songs, and sometimes this way they view their problems.

2. Nature speaks of the Almighty and credible attributes of God. Even man, animals, broth, and creation in its entirely makes man inexcusable, therefore only a fool would say there is no God.

CONCLUSION

GOD'S WAYS AND MAN'S WAYS

God's way is better than any other. Man has a very distorted view of life and its reality; until man comes to full realization of this misdemeanor and corrects this error, they can never come to 100 percent fulfilment of who they ought to be: gods, little Jesus, the sons of God. The truth in this case is that man does not have a way of his or her own. Man was created to serve God. And the opposite of serving God is going away from God. The territory of those who refuse to serve God, whether man, woman, children, angels, or demons, is the way of perdition.

But we are gods. Jesus is our way, our truth, and our life. We are not children of perdition. We are children of light and not children of darkness. Jesus is our master, our friend, brother, mentor and Lord. We are one with him. Alleluia. We are of God, born of God, cloned of God. Therefore, we are gods. Yes, we are gods. Amen. Praise God, our Father.

www.ingramcontent.com/pod-product-compliance
Lightning Source LLC
Chambersburg PA
CBHW060323130626
46553CB00003B/894